A Doubter's Guide to God

by

Roger Martin

Copyright © 2016 by Roger Martin
All rights reserved

Woodley Press
Washburn University
Topeka, Kansas

Cover photograph: Glacier National Park

Book design: Pam LeRow

Published in the United States of America
ISBN: 978-0-9908128-3-8
Library of Congress Control Number: 2016932965

First Edition

9 8 7 6 5 4 3 2 First Printing

Dedication

To Barbara, with whom I shared a hymnal
on my first day at Peace Mennonite Church,
by whose subtle promptings I chose to become a
member of that church, and to whom I am gratefully
committed for her virtues, one of those being her
capacity for enduring my flaws.

CONTENTS

Prologue

God is not known, he is not understood, he is used – sometimes as meat purveyor, sometimes as moral support, sometimes as friend, sometimes as an object of love.

James Henry Leuba
"The Contents of Religious Consciousness"
The Monist

I have no living sense of commerce with a God. I envy those who have, for I know that the addition of such a sense would help me greatly.

William James
from a letter to James Henry Leuba

1.

The Wager

You would like to attain faith, and do not know the way; you would like to cure yourself of unbelief, and ask the remedy for it. Learn of those who have been bound like you . . . . Follow the way by which they began; by acting as if they believed. . . .

Blaise Pascal
Pensées

I begin in *medias res* – the middle of things – or perhaps, more accurately, the muddle. As Jesse Jackson said at the 1984 Democratic Convention, after having made a racial slur against Jews, "God's not finished with me yet." I am so unfinished a spiritual product that I wonder, at times, whether God's even *started* – or, for that matter, what the word "God" points to. In fact, please bracket the word *God* with quotation marks when you see it in the pages that follow. I use the word in some sense other than the familiar – rock of ages, shelter from the storm, a buckler (whatever that is), a light at the end of a tunnel, a father, a king and so on. I'm not sure what the sense is, but it's not, to be precise, any of those.

•

Why should anyone pursue a God the senses can't grasp? who, as a force for good, hardly seems to matter, if we judge by the actions of God's signature creation, *Homo sapiens*? whose earthly reps often muster a following by whipping up a frenzy of ill feeling toward one or another group? Why would anyone mess with a God who rails throughout the Old Testament against his human betrayers – then dispatches a son to redeem us? A son who, like the father, is betrayed? whose most characteristic action, in the closing days of his life, is inaction? whose "brand" is crucifixion? Why would any thinking man or woman, knowing this, make a leap of faith?

I didn't leap. Haven't leaped. But I can imagine the talk among my longtime friends about my decision to put a toe into the waters of organized religion. They'd seen me through the chart-casting (Virgo sun, Scorpio moon, Libra rising), Tarot card-reading and I Ching-throwing phases. They'd humored me during my oneirological phase – the years of feverish dream study – by gathering together for Dream Club once a month. I've been working to crack the code of the mysterious *something* at the heart of life for as long as I've lived, so when I plunged back into religion at age 51 it should have surprised no one. On the other hand, I can imagine shock when people heard I was attending Peace Mennonite Church in Lawrence, Kansas.

Martin, a MENNONITE? Are you kidding?

I guessed that my friends would want no part of my foolishness. They'd all been chewed on enough by organized religion, thank you. I'm lucky that they didn't challenge my choice to re-engage. I was a little wary of it, too.

•

My loss-of-faith story is unexceptional. High school: I grow disillusioned with the politics of my church. (The civil rights movement was not embraced by Bethel Evangelical and Reformed Church.) University freshman year: I feel ignored by a Christ whom I barrage, to no effect, with gimme prayers. His silence in response to my pain is the last straw. My mother's religious convictions, acquired from her dad, the Rev. Albert Katterjohn, a pastor in Wright City, Missouri, prove no shield.

But the erosion of faith had begun earlier. In fifth grade, I scored 135 on an I.Q. test and was labeled "gifted." I was transferred to a different school, where I was assigned to a classroom filled with North St. Louis kids, most of them working class, who'd also scored well. Back in the hood, Sal Mattina, who became a fireman and never left St. Louis, started calling me *The Brain.* Sal didn't know my I.Q. was in the bottom third of my class (we riffled through the teacher's drawer one day and found the scores), but I did, and, to compensate, studied furiously. There was plenty to study. William Kottmeyer, assistant superintendent of elementary and special schools in the St. Louis public school system, articulated the reason for our hefty homework load in a commentary that ran in the *St. Louis Post-Dispatch* in January 1958: "Many of these pupils have already become accustomed to getting good grades with a minimum of effort, have developed poor study habits and dash off academic chores indifferently. In classrooms in which the competition is lively and stimulating, the standards high and exacting, there are preliminary howls of indignation at taxing homework assignments, and of anguish when the first report cards are issued." Taxing, yes: hours of homework a day. Just about the same time I entered the program, the Russians launched Sputnik. As prospective intellectual elites, we would help defend the nation from Nikita Khrushchev and Red China, from the massing of nuclear warheads against us in Cuba and later the toppling of dominoes across Southeast Asia.

As a spur, our teacher, the tall and besuited Mr. Ramsey, a lover of Richard Wagner's *Ring of the Nibelung*, read the class rankings aloud at the end of each semester. I was driven by I.Q. shame and helped by the mania I got from Dad. He spent much of World War II in an ammo dump in England and came home with his nerves shot. His shop down in the cellar was the medium for his nervous energy, the place he made a wagon for my brother and me, built a lab bench for my chemistry set, carved a face into a bowling pin and transformed it into a lamp. Books and study helped me to ground my intensity, and my mind was a safe haven during those spells when Dad came apart, winding into a frenzied activity or dropping into an impenetrable gloom.

My first girlfriend tried to argue me into Buddhism in our senior year in high school, but it didn't work: I clung to Christ. At the university, that ended. My first major was anthropology, and I was excited by the concept of cultural relativism. I read this in *Cultural and Social Anthropology: Selected Readings*, edited by Peter B. Hammond: "It is ideology, not religion, that is universal. The beliefs of the atheistic humanist, the nihilist, and the agnostic can be just as strongly held and provide sources of satisfaction and security at least analogous to those derived from religious conviction." The words lifted me to a vantage point from which my previous faith appeared provincial, childish. Later I read Nietzsche and warmed to Albert Camus. When *Time* magazine published its famous "Is God Dead?" cover in 1966, I knew the answer. Being a humanist-agnostic seemed the only intellectually respectable choice.

I remember walking one day into a laundromat and coming across a tract written by Bill Bright, founder of the Campus Crusade for Christ, titled, "Have you heard of the FOUR SPIRITUAL LAWS?" Here's Law No. 1: "God loves you and offers a wonderful plan for your life." Given my undiagnosed depression (the dark side of my father's mania, and mine) and my rage at the social order (this was the mid-1960s and there was plenty to rage about), I found Bright's bland assurances one more reason to be disgusted with Christianity.

My turning away was predictable: "High cognitive ability predicts high religious involvement in high school, followed in young adulthood by a time of questioning that often prompts changes in religious affiliation and/or apostasy," write Marjorie Lindner Gunnoe and Kristin A. Moore in an article published in 2002 in the *Journal for the Scientific Study of Religion*, "Predictors of Religiosity Among Youth Aged 17-22."

•

What brings people back to the search for God? You don't wander into church after a 32-year timeout for the potluck dinners. Strike that: Some people do. Others return because of nostalgia, still others, guilt or shame. Sometimes it has to do with kids, I understand: I've never had any. Sometimes, the reason is more indeterminate – the old fierce pull of blood – sometimes, narrow: a crisis. Or, as in my case, *crises*.

There's too much else to do in life, too much that's far more amusing, or at least less tasking, than thinking about the unthinkable, about a God who, if s/he/it exists, may hide, or else disappoint in other ways. Most people sitting in church probably aren't there to ponder the *Deus absconditus* – the hidden and unknowable God. I assume they show up to deal with the thinkable God, the one with plans for their lives, the one who answers prayer (though not always as we'd like), the census-taker of the hairs on our heads.

In fact, research shows that rather than being made in God's image, we make God in ours, and the kind of God we imagine has much to do with our race, our gender, the geographic region we inhabit and our education. Two Baylor University professors, in an article that appeared in 2007 in the *Journal for the Scientific Study of Religion*, wrote that though 96 percent of Americans "indicate some level of belief . . . in God," there is an "underlying diversity of opinion" about God's character. In their study, Paul Froese and Christopher Bader theorized that two characteristics of God, in particular, are up for grabs – how much God 1. is involved with the world and 2. judges human behavior. Having surveyed 1,729 people, they found that women, compared with the average, thought God more engaged but less judgmental. Southerners saw God as more engaged AND judgmental. The God of nonwhites was more judgmental than the God of any other demographic. And those with some college see God "both as less judgmental and less involved in the world than average."

The in-your-face God is far more imaginable to most people than a hands-off God: "Approximately 15.6 percent of the sample scored the highest possible score on God's engagement, compared to the less than 1 percent (0.8 percent) who view God in the most distant terms."

•

I've been in the hunt for nearly 20 years (this time), and though God still isn't thinkable the search itself helps. Acting like a Christian – by going to church Sunday mornings, serving on committees, scouring the research literature on religion, participating in contemplative prayer with others, reading the written testimonials of the wisest and most nuanced minds out there trying to make sense of the extrasensory most high, washing dishes once a month at the soup kitchen for the homeless – is changing me.

Slowly.

Church is still hard. Whenever two or more people gather together, you get in-groups and out-groups, and, typically, un-Christian stuff starts to happen. In a Christian setting, the pain inflicted by this behavior is acute, the irony cruel.

Nevertheless, I think I have become a (marginally) better soul for my engagement. Of course I still honk when somebody crosses two lanes to make a right turn in front of me; but I tend to notice now when I'm ill-tempered. (And when I cross two lanes and somebody else lays on the horn, I mouth the word "Sorry" to the screaming face in the other car.) To *notice* these things is a start.

I'd like to pull God on stage for a round of applause, but he's apparently not into making personal appearances for me. Or maybe he thinks my efforts have been too paltry, their results too few, and this isn't the county fair, after all, where everybody gets a blue ribbon for every little thing, even if the hairs on their heads *are* numbered. Maybe God also suspects, rightly, that my desire to have him come out and take a bow is just some conniving on my part to get him to make an appearance.

•

I have lost my anger toward religion. Age has brought a yearning. I want both my broken self and the broken world to be repaired. That's one reason why I've decided to make Blaise Pascal's pragmatic wager that God exists. I do this despite Simone Weil's objection, in *Waiting for God*, that "Pascal's method seems to me one of the worst for attaining faith." For me, though, Pascal's is a way into faith that doesn't violate the intellect. Besides, Pascal's "way" involves stubborn will, my strong suit.

Pascal, a 17th century French mathematician and physicist, wrote in *Pensées*: "It is incomprehensible that God should exist, and it is incomprehensible that He should not exist." He argues that because reason cannot decide the case, and because the odds are 50-50, one should wager God exists. He writes: "Let us weigh the gain and the loss in wagering that God is. Let us estimate these two chances. If you gain, you gain all; if you lose, you lose nothing. Wager, then, without hesitation that He is."

Pascal is vulnerable to attack. The wonderful-plan Christians will find his approach oddly cerebral, if not downright vulgar, given the casino metaphor. On the other hand, those who feel that Christianity blighted their early years may argue that there is not "everything to gain" from belief. Bliss is not faith's inevitable trickledown.

Moreover, lots of folks consider belief in God a blunting of intellectual integrity at best, and a *willed* belief, of the sort Pascal recommends, as little more than willed self-deception. Besides all this, there are ample reasons, as I've already said, for disgust with God's associates here on Earth: the Crusaders, the Spanish Inquisitors, the orchestrators of the Salem witch trials, the fallen televangelists, the sexually predatory priests, the terrorists. And I'll say this again, too, so you won't regard what I'm telling you as so much Pollyannaish spew: When spiritual minds catch the legalism virus, look out. They'll hurt you. Still, I bet the average Christian is less evil than frail, less mean than frightened.

Even other pragmatists find fault with Pascal. Psychologist William James found the Pascalian approach "mechanical." In "The Will to Believe," an address delivered to clubs at Yale and Brown universities in the mid 1890s, James said:

"We feel that a faith in masses and holy water adopted willfully after such a mechanical calculation [as Pascal's] would lack the inner soul of faith's reality; and if we were ourselves in the place of the Deity, we should probably take particular pleasure in cutting off believers of this pattern from their infinite reward. . . . The talk of our believing by our volition seems, then, from one point of view, simply silly. From another point of view it is worse than silly, it is vile."

While Pascal focused on the potential gains or losses in an afterlife from making (or refusing) a leap of faith, James argued for a more immediate payoff, which he summarizes in Lecture 20 of his *Varieties of Religious Experience*. He writes that the "psychological characteristics" of religion include "a new zest which adds itself like a gift to life" and "an assurance of safety and a temper of peace, and, in relation to others, a preponderance of loving affections."

Zest? Assurance of safety? Those haven't been among my gains, at least so far. But a temper of peace and an increase in loving affection – yes, on my best days, I experience more of these than before.

At one point, in an essay titled "Is Life Worth Living?" James writes "Believe that life *is* worth living, and your belief will help create the fact." When we will to believe that God exists and acts as a force of love among us and other life forms, and when we then join others who share that belief, and together put our shoulders to the wheel, we may help to birthe a better planet.

•

In sum, I'm less interested in the documented failings of Christians than in the prospects for individuals raised, as I was, in the Christian tradition, but who've fallen away, to re-commit themselves to reinvestigating the Christian story and to become conduits by which Christ energy enters the world. For religion to come to ground requires thinking, feeling and self-conscious human agents who construct religious ideals from a welter of (sometimes contradictory) possibilities and then embody these in word and deed. Tall order? Yes. But it's OK. The story of Christianity – or Islam or Hinduism – is one that is written life by life (that is, drop by drop).

When I talk about our becoming conduits for Christ energy, I sound like a Mennonite (more later about that) with a twist of Gnosticism. Before Christianity became *organized* (with the help of its powerful convert, the Roman emperor Constantine in the early fourth century), the gnostics put faith in the *individual* religious imagination. Elaine Pagels, in *The Gnostic Gospels*, writes that "gnostics considered original creative invention to be the mark of anyone who becomes spiritually alive. Each one, like students of a painter or writer, expected to express his own perceptions by revising and transforming what he was taught." One of Gnosticism's legacies has been a fear among the orthodox of the threat posed by the individual imagination to organized religion. Not without reason. Anarchy, self-indulgence and just-plain strangeness can result from individuals making a little too free with their Christianity, with leaving the Round Table and going off on grail quests.

On the other hand, the trouble with the repression of the individual imagination is the pressure this selectively exerts against the engagement in religion of imaginative people. Pagels mentions Valentinius, William Blake, Rembrandt van Rijn, Fyodor Dostoevsky and Leo Tolstoy, among others, as returning again and again to Christian symbols "to express their own experience. And yet they found themselves in revolt against orthodox institutions. An increasing number of people today share their experience."

Moreover, when it comes to belief "systems," there's plenty of freelancing going on. Ninety-nine percent of those who identified themselves as *Christians* in a Lou Harris poll a few years ago said they believed in God; but 22 percent of those also believed in reincarnation. Just what IS a

Christian, if nearly a quarter of them harbor Hindu ideas? Who's kidding whom? The Christian establishment, under pressure from science and other social forces, is subject to enormous fluctuations of sentiment within short time spans. According to a Pew Forum on Religion and Public Life, two of three people in 1963 believed the Bible was the actual word of God; by 1999, the number had dropped to one in three. What does it mean to be "Christian" when understanding of the sacred text changes so radically in so little time?

It seems inevitable that as the internetting of the world continues, Christianity will be salted with the Dalai Lama and peppered with Buddha. Heterodoxy happens; get used to it. Will Christianity morph, as a result? Perhaps. On the other hand, it may also firm up its identity by examining what it does and doesn't share in common with other faiths. Besides, there's a chance here for a reformation, an opportunity to re-envision Christianity.

•

I may seem doctrinally suspect, but I'm not bent on evicting Christ from church and replacing him with some kind of refried New Age quantum mechanical booga-booga. I don't see the face of God in redwood trees, though perhaps when I see my first one later this year I will. (Actually, I think trying to put a face on "God" is part of the problem, not a solution, but that's another essay.)

What I'm looking for, personally, is a better bond with Christianity and Christians. I can hear the objection: *You don't take Christianity's measure, my good fellow; Christianity takes yours*. Practically speaking, I don't think that position is workable. There needs to be give and take.

Some years ago, I helped teach a Sunday school class for teenagers at Peace Mennonite. My co-teacher was a much more orthodox Christian, so we did a good cop/bad cop thing with the kids. I played the good cop, the liberal who isn't bound by tradition. One Sunday I told the group, "There is no way to know that God exists or does not exist. I was for years the kind of agnostic, who, confronted with not knowing, gives up the search. That's a reasonable choice. Today, I'm an agnostic who searches. I pray. I come to this church, help teach this class – and act as if God exists."

I was trying to make breathing room in the church for young skeptics. The same day I said: "I act as if God exists because I am convinced that even if that's not true, the world may be the tiniest bit better if I do that. That's because I assume that believing in God requires I be more loving. Perhaps the love will spread. The world will start to heal when we are warmer toward each other."

I hadn't read Pascal or James at that point, so I wasn't cribbing from them – scout's honor. And I didn't address the great confound: the complexity of love, which isn't so much about feeling as it is dogged determination. I didn't talk, either, about the guilt by association that comes of being a Christian – the judgment and spite that sometimes follow when Christianity and politics enter into an unholy alliance. And I did not say how deflated I felt when I learned, at their age, that religion and human imperfection – an imperfection characterized by an inability to see the log in one's own eye but never miss the mote in another's – are inseparable.

I did not say, because I didn't want to overload them, *Look kids, being a Christian will put you up against the wall. Loving humans and loving God are both hard. You don't "earn" love in either case, no matter how many good deeds you do or how many weeds you pull out of your soul. There's a chemistry involved in loving a person or loving God, and in the long run much more: Faith cannot be attained without a willed motion of the heart toward God – but it also requires, according to orthodox belief, anyway, God's leveraging your efforts with grace.* Nor did I say, *When I pray, it often feels like I'm tossing coins into an abyss whose bottom I can't see. I don't know whether I should be asking, listening, or what.* They'll learn all that on their own, unless they're among those for whom faith is easy.

•

My as-if commitment helps me understand those who get weak in the knees thinking about leaps of faith. And my spiritual wobbliness helps me appreciate the many paths that lead people to feelings of "religious" awe – the flow experience, the world of dreams, love's euphoria, and, yes, redwood trees.

Yet I continue to TRY to think and act as if God exists. In doing so, I honor my grandfather and my late mother, a humble and self-described goody-two-shoes who nevertheless seemed to pack plenty of steel in her soul.

Lately, reading through her diaries, I found she had her share of dark nights, some of them brought on by the collapse of my faith after leaving home. On Thanksgiving Day, 1965, she wrote, "Sadly, I did not go to church [today] to show the gratitude I feel for our <u>many</u> blessings. Will I ever get through this doubting stage in my Christian growth? Today I feel a glimmer of truth. Roger has planted serious seeds of doubt within me – but I feel it is a time of testing. I cannot pooh-pooh 2,000 years and millions of souls and minds."

Apparently, the doubts persisted for a while. In a letter I wrote in March 1968, which she saved, I recommended Soren Kierkegaard to her – a serious bit of pretending on my part, given that I'd barely nicked the surface of his difficult prose – "if you are still in the midst of a sort of religious crisis." I see now, reading further into my letter, that I was already coming to a Pascalian or Jamesian position. This happened by way of Kierkegaard, whom I summarized this way in the letter: "His whole [emphasis] is on faith – [not] on some kind of God-out-there. In order for God to be real, you don't try to understand him objectively and intellectually. Rather, you just commit yourself and your energy to him. Your faith becomes stronger because there is a tension between the objective uncertainty of God and the subjective reality of him to you. The more committed you are to God, the more real and 'true' he becomes . . . ."

Objective uncertainty and subjective reality? This language sounds suspiciously as if it has been lifted from class notes. Besides the sophomoric touches – parroting my professors and pretentiously lecturing my mother despite my lack of life experience – there's the hypocrisy of my handing out a recipe for meeting God decades before I tried it myself. Using my mother as a prop, I was trying to send myself a message. I was 22 and didn't grasp the truth of what I wrote. Out of the mouths of babes.

So it is commitment, not "knowing," that keeps me on the faith trail. Does the "fact" or "fiction" of God matter so long as the result is love? (Conversely, if the result of a belief in God as an inescapable fact is contempt for others, rather than love, what sort of "God" is *that*?) I have no answers, but I can bear witness: The world is broken and stress and sadness appear to be more basic, more universal, than joy. I also believe there is enough mystery to suggest the wisdom of doubt. Even though doubt carries risks (paralysis or despair), it also can produce a tentativeness that provides space for other people and their beliefs. That's my wager.

Hard Years

2.

An Addict

I here present you, courteous reader, with the record of a remarkable period of my life. . . . I trust that it will prove, not merely an interesting record, but, in a considerable degree, instructive. In that hope it is that I have drawn it up; and that must be my apology for breaking through those restraints of delicate reserve, which, for the most part, intercept the public exposure of our own errors and infirmities.

Thomas De Quincey
1821 Preface
Confessions of an English Opium-Eater

About those crises that drove me back to church.

If you've seen the dark side – the pitch black side – they will seem trivial. In the language of Alcoholics Anonymous, and other recovery groups, I hit a high bottom, not a low one. I can picture myself at a table with a bunch of beat-up-looking, cigarette-smoking, coffee-sipping men and women. The 12-step meeting is about to begin.

Those years I dropped out of church I was a spiritual corpse and an emotional mess, I tell them. *Running on fumes (actually, marijuana smoke). I also learned I was excessively dependent on (addicted to?) trying to fix broken people, specifically, women people. In fact, I'd bet that I needed to help them much more than they needed to be helped.*

People join recovery programs when they've lost control and know it. Among alcoholics, the urge is to booze; among drug users, to toke or geeze; among those who are labeled codependents, there is a compulsion to help those who don't want, or can't receive, help. Pot and broken women were my addictions. I clung to both.

One of the early gurus of codependency, Melody Beattie, wrote in her book *Codependent No More* that a codependent is someone "who has let another person's behavior affect him or her, and who is obsessed with controlling that person's behavior." The word "affect" doesn't do justice, I think, to the galvanizing attractiveness, to the codependent person, of a person who seems to need fixing. My therapist used to ask, jokingly, "Have you been driving the ambulance for anybody this week?"

I never went to Narcotics Anonymous with my pot problem, but I did go to Codependents Anonymous (called CODA by insiders) trying to understand and repair my sometimes-flawed people-picker, as well as to soothe the florid grief that followed relationship collapse. One day after a CODA meeting, someone came up and said I needed to *get a sponsor*. A sponsor is somebody you can call should you feel yourself slipping into a craving – in my case, into a craving for contact with some poor soul who really, really didn't want me comin' around. A sponsor is a combination of probation officer and therapist, someone who is managing a comeback from the addiction in question. A lot of people grow inside these programs, but once it hit the sponsorship stage, I bolted. In my life myth, I was the counselor, not the counselee.

Besides, the language of recovery programs is slogan-heavy. In the spirit of Nike's *Just do it*, recovery groups want you to *keep it simple, one day at a time*, by coming to grips with your *stinkin' thinkin'* and *turning it over to a higher power* to deal with. I resist using aphorisms to guide my life – although, God knows, I've tried. I once spent about nine or 10 days in a hotel becoming a certified Avatar®. That's the first stage of initiation for those who join the Avatar® program, and who sign documents swearing they'll keep what goes on a secret (which was part, but only part, of what put me off). The three-word nugget of truth for an Avatar® is that "Beliefs create experiences." A couple of my brightest friends promoted the course to me after taking advanced courses and becoming Masters and then Wizards. I find this memory painful. Of course beliefs create experiences – but so do the conditions of your birth, your mood when you wake up in the morning, genes, accident and what you had for lunch.

Christians, of course, also offer three-word guides to truth – and my reaction to those is the same. "God is love," someone says. Pair that with the notion that humans are made in God's image and I think, *Well, there's a lot of non-love in this world, isn't there? Is God, then, NOT present in unloving people? Is his occupancy of our experience so partial?*

The problem is that from being dismissive of the apothegms of any belief system it's just a short step to dismissing the system itself.

Thomas De Quincey, the 19th century author of *Confessions of an English Opium Eater*, wrote that "to meditate too much and to observe too little" had tripped him up, easing the slide into addiction. I get that. Had I been more observant, I might, for example, have noticed early on that addicts are, much like self-help groups and religions, good at wielding the short sentence to defend their addiction.

Why toke? you ask.

Why not? I answer. *Been a hard week.*

I don't know how big my denial was back then or is today. But I do believe that within the labyrinth of self-accusation and self-defense of my wounded inner addict is a grail self, one capable of wonder, excitement and mischief. Perhaps that's romantic humbug, yet sometimes, I think, I catch glimpses of this self.

I'll start by talking about the marijuana rather than the codependency (a word that I use as an umbrella to describe my relationship ills and that I mistrust). In doing so, I'll borrow from De Quincey an apology "for breaking through those restraints of delicate reserve, which, for the most part, intercept the public exposure of our own errors and infirmities."

•

At 21, in 1967, I smoked marijuana for the first time. I was returning from a few days spent on the West Coast during the Summer of Love, wearing no flowers in my hair and with no appetite to sleep in Golden Gate Park, ever again, given the cold, drizzly night we'd put in there. I and two friends (who'd had the sense to sleep in the car that night while I was outside, shivering in my sleeping bag on the cold ground) made the return trip by driving through the desert Southwest toward Dallas. There, we spent an evening at the home of an acquaintance, a girl going to Southern Methodist University. That's also where Jerry, a hitchhiker we'd picked up on the coast, turned us on. The result, as is often the case for first-time tokers: I got sleepy and lay down on the couch to rest as the others went up on the roof to look at the night sky.

At 26, I became a daily pot smoker. Reaching full-blown dependency or addiction seems to require, for some, an incubation period. De Quincey, for example, was an intermittent opium eater for almost a decade before plunging into daily use. I still don't know whether to call my relationship with marijuana an *addiction*. Pot is not heroin, meth, cocaine or nicotine. You don't get withdrawals when you stop smoking it. Quitting a four-pack-a-day cigarette addiction was more difficult.

Even as I ripened into a daily user, I, along with most others in my generation, scorned the label "addiction" applied to marijuana. An American Medical Association Council on Scientific Affairs report dated 2001 contained a section titled "Adverse Effects of Marijuana." Amid a host of bad news appears this admission: "Although dependent on the setting, marijuana can cause relaxation and enhance mood. Ordinary sensory experiences may be intensified, with increased talkativeness, perceptual alterations, and distortion in time sense . . . ." If I wrote a book about my marijuana years, I'd put that description in the chapter titled *Toking: The First 30 Minutes*. That slice of the experience was such fun that it diverted my attention, for years, from the less pleasant phases.

The same AMA report spoke of 4 to 9 percent of marijuana users becoming substance-dependent. I believe I fell into that category. Recently, the *New York Times* ran a series about why marijuana should be legalized at the federal level. In an article headlined "What Science Says About Marijuana," Philip Boffey reported that the drug "isn't addictive in the same sense as heroin, from which withdrawal is an agonizing, physical ordeal. But it can interact with pleasure centers in the brain and can create a strong sense of psychological dependence that addiction experts say can be very difficult to break."

Ditto.

•

After De Quincey became a daily user, there were still times, he writes, when he drastically diminished his daily dose, only to see it rise later. That wasn't my pattern with marijuana. After years of daily use, I finally dropped back to weekend use, but I quit only after I was arrested.

More about that later. Here I'll just say that after the Kansas Bureau of Investigation agents left my house, I lay awake till 4 having a dream that's as bad as it gets for someone like me. It was a waking dream, composed of a single sound: the one you hear in movies when they slam the jail door shut. In our family, my brother had cornered the market on lawbreaking during a rebellious adolescence. Now, with the bust, the outlaw thing in me would be outed, I thought.

Dreams can, like religious conversion, be a powerful source of sobriety. De Quincey reports quitting opium after his 18-year use – and eight years of abuse – because of horrible dreams.

The opium eater "lies under a world's weight of incubus and nightmare," he writes. At one point, he was besieged by "oriental dreams": "Thousands of years I lived and was buried in stone coffins, with mummies and sphinxes, in narrow chambers at the heart of eternal pyramids. I was kissed, with cancerous kisses by crocodiles, and was laid, confounded with all unutterable abortions, among reeds and Nilotic mud."

A low bottom indeed.

•

For years, I was trapped between two lives: In one I was a backyard grower and pothead, in the other an editor of an award-winning university research magazine, composer of tag lines for multimillion dollar university capital campaigns, and ghost editor of a collection of essays submitted by presidents and chancellors of universities and compiled by our campus CEO. The tension between these roles was both exciting and unnerving.

Smoking marijuana took the edges off, helping to remedy a problem – edginess – it had helped in part to create. A therapist once labeled me an "agitated depressive," which seems to have been De Quincey's thing, too. At one point in *Confessions* he writes of being troubled by "nervous irritation." At another he describes a "profound melancholy" emanating from liver problems leading him to an apothecary, a "comatose old gentleman" who was "careless of his own practice" and stood "under that painfully necessity . . . of seeking his remuneration in excessive deluges of medicine." For De Quincey, the apothecary selected "one horrid mixture that must have suggested itself to him when prescribing for a tiger": opium.

My drug of choice turned me into a pussy cat. Smoking pot conferred a calm that some people get when praying, on nature hikes, at the Zen center, on 10-K runs or at stress-management workshops. These days, people also take Prozac or Zoloft or Paxil or Wellbutrin to achieve that calm. I started taking legal drugs after the bust, back in 1996. I use a cocktail of generic versions of Zoloft, Wellbutrin and Adderall, which, together, bestow a calm (though not the pleasure) that formerly was available to me only when smoking marijuana. But mood regulators without too many side effects didn't reach market till the late 1980s. A doctor I told about my daily marijuana habit in 1979 offered me Valium as a substitute. I said, "All that'd do is give me two addictions." Having said all this, I don't condemn pot smoking. Most folks handle it fine.

I was married for 17 years to an artist, and in the '70s we had a fantasy that I would write while she painted and somehow the money would take care of itself. I taught freshman English, part-time, at the university and she carried mail, part-time, on a rural route. I'd write an occasional essay for the local underground rag or co-write, with a friend, mock news articles for a parody of screamer tabloids called the *City Moon*. I always wrote stoned, but I didn't write with discipline or focus. I just fooled around.

•

After you dance with a drug for a long time, the relationship gets complicated. De Quincey started his romance with opium by using it once every three weeks, on Tuesday or Saturday nights, to enhance his enjoyment of the opera and afterward to take sallies around London, eavesdropping on the poor in marketplaces. It did not make him torpid, he writes. In fact, it helped him sustain his otherwise drooping "animal energies" 'round the clock. But years later he stopped exercising and fell into "total sedentariness."

Over the course of time, my relationship to pot also evolved. The chapter I've already described, about the first-half hour of the high, was fun. Getting high was like taking a machete to the jungle of worry and fear that sprouted within me with lush vigor.

The chapter titled *Pot: Growing It* was less fun. It had its adventurous and daring aspects, especially because I always grew plants in my yard and, until the end, within the city limits. (Good fences make good neighbors.) But then there was the day a city commissioner from whom I was renting, who lived next door to the rental, came over while I happened to be tripping and commented: "Pretty nice looking pot plants you've got there." They numbered around 40.

Then, one morning I awoke to find a number of those plants stolen, creating a mandatory, hurried harvest.

And, years later, there was the afternoon when a fireman came to the house because I was illegally burning vines in a backyard pit. Unfortunately, four lush pot plants were growing right next to the pit. Just as he was about to leave (either ignoring the plants or failing to recognize them) a policeman arrived to look the scene over. After they'd both left, there was a hasty harvest. I piled the stash into a garbage sack and took it to the home of a friend whose first question, when I explained the situation, was a sensible one: "Did they follow you?"

The cops never came back. I don't know why, nor do I know how I made it right, in my mind, to keep on growing after that. But I did.

Then there was an unpleasant chapter titled *Pot: The Hangover*. At the time, I wasn't moderate in my use of pot or alcohol. Only when the wheels came off my closest friendship, in the late 1980s, did I see a therapist for the first time in years and become a weekend user.

•

Addicts tend to be faithful to their substance of choice. They can usually tell you why their addiction is preferable to some other. For example, De Quincey goes to lengths belittling alcohol. "Wine constantly leads a man to the brink of absurdity and extravagance," he writes and will, past a certain point, "disperse the intellectual energies." Opium "always seems to compose what had been agitated, and to concentrate what had been distracted." Moreover, the opium eater feels the "diviner part of his nature," he says, referring to himself as the Pope of the true church of opium.

I and a good many potheads tend to a similar view. We would deride, for example, those who drank too much, and I still tend to believe that pot is less perilous than alcohol, a position taken by the Gray Lady (aka the *New York Times*) in its endorsement of federal legalization in July 2014. One alcoholic I know who goes to AA meetings said, "I knew it was going to kill me." So he stopped. Another friend, who took Antabuse to make himself sick when he drank, in an effort to disown alcohol, wrote to me about his second day of quitting booze: "There I was, trucking down the sunny side of Sobriety Street late afternoon when suddenly it's ice under my feet, darkness falling all around and scary ice-cracking sounds. I scurried home and crawled under the desk – my safe place – and waited for the weather to clear." The wait lasted several hours.

I never had those kinds of experiences with pot, never thought it would kill me. A toke or two would blunt what De Quincey labeled "nervous irritation." Rolling down life's highways, it felt in those days as if there were a rock wedged in my tire treads. Ker-bump, ker-bump, ker-bump. Really annoying. The first glorious hit of marijuana dissolved the rock, smoothed the ride.

Trouble is, one toke never seemed like enough.

A therapist once asked me the benefits of getting high. I told him it helped me stop tapdancing, stop thinking so hard, stop talking so incessantly – ker-bump, ker-bump, ker-bump. Stoners weren't expected to give much, I told him, not the ass-busting 200 percent I thought I had to give to be an acceptable human being.

"It feels good to be at the bottom of the pit, doesn't it?" he said.

•

I traded my four-pack-a-day cigarette habit for a one-joint-a-day habit on April 20, 1972. It seemed reasonable, given that I kept a burning cigarette at hand as I ate, smoked when I woke from sleep, smoked even when I was feverish and coughing. It also seemed reasonable to say I couldn't really write well unless I was high – that I couldn't find those wonderful ideas and words. It seemed reasonable to have sex only after I was high because, straight, I couldn't get that limber-as-cooked-spaghetti feeling in my limbs, couldn't make my mind and self-consciousness disappear. It seemed reasonable to be nervous about going home to visit my parents. After all, that would mean not toking for 72 hours. A horrible shock to the system.

It seemed reasonable to empty a ballpoint pen and stuff it with a couple of joints so I wouldn't be without pot when I vacationed in Mexico in 1978. Yes, I actually smuggled dope INTO Mexico. What about the risk of Mexican jail time? No problemo!

It seemed reasonable to sneak away from work and drive around till I found streets without traffic or pedestrians so I could light up, roll down the windows of the car and blow the smoke out (fearing, all the time, I would stink of reefer when I returned to work – but then, as I got high, forgetting the fear). How else, but stoned, could I write award-winning prose?

And then it seemed reasonable, once I learned that cultivating fewer than five plants in Kansas meant you'd be charged only with a misdemeanor, not a felony, to grow four or fewer a year. That way, if I ever got busted, I'd walk. How hard could diversion be compared with jail time?

Addiction permits the most remarkable absurdities to flourish in one's thinking. De Quincey, for example, argues that eating opium promotes a nearly invisible perspiring in addicts. He tells of a glow that would appear on the face of opium-eating poet Samuel Taylor Coleridge. De Quincey also contends that opium probably saved him from the tuberculosis that killed his father.

The substance breeds dependency by making one feel that the state of mind it produces is the ground state . . . home . . . the place one ought to occupy, to which one is *entitled.* De Quincey writes that when he was high, "it seemed to me . . . I stood at a distance, aloof from the uproar of life; as if the tumult, the fever, and the strife, were suspended; a respite were granted from the secret burdens of the heart; some Sabbath of repose; some resting from human labors."

It allowed him to experience his grail self, the innocence and detachment of an infant. Religious people also long for that; when it comes, they call it grace. In this way, the substance abuser and the spiritually fervent person are not so different.

•

I was growing two plants the year of the bust. The day it happened, my wife called me at work – a plane had been circling the house, low. I drove home fast. When I arrived, the Kansas Bureau of Investigation agents already were there. A couple of them babysat us while a couple of others drove away to look for a judge who would sign a search warrant letting them into the house. An unreal day. At one point, an agent who seemed to be the leader, sitting with me in the drowsy hours of the afternoon, said, "You don't know what a pleasure it is to deal with folks like you. You go to a meth lab where somebody has automatic weapons . . . well, you don't know what you'll run into." *I bet we're the nicest criminals you've met all summer*, I thought, *maybe in your whole life.*

I tried to be neighborly, as if they were drop-in guests. I talked with one about a book I was writing, focused on the stock market and investment. He talked about the retirement program the agents were enrolled in – how pitiful it was. He joked, quietly, that some of the guys were too dumb to realize it. Another agent mentioned a throat polyp. The biopsy results would be finished soon, and he was clearly scared. The marijuana plants got rave reviews: One agent said they were the best they'd seen all summer. *Maybe this is how it is between prison guards and inmates,* I thought, *when things go well.*

The two plants weighed 23 pounds, according to the arrest report. Anybody who's ever grown weed will realize the absurdity of this number. It was inflated by weighing everything – stalk, limbs, clay on the roots – not just the smokable part. That drove up the fine, which was established by weight. (They asked for the money to pay the fine – around $10,000 – on the spot, which I guess was their way of seeing whether I had salted drug money around the house in jars and under mattresses. I said I didn't have that kind of cash, but I tendered an olive branch. I called Fidelity Investment and handed the phone to an officer. An automated voice told him how much cash I had in a money-market fund, assuring the agents that I would be able to cover the fine.)

Eventually, I sweet-talked my way inside the house – to pee, I said. While that was true, I also managed to ditch a couple of peyote cactus which I'd had growing in planters, strictly for ornament, for years. They were gifts from friends, but had they been busted, too, things could have gotten much uglier.

I had been mistaken about the threshold of a felony related to marijuana. The heaviest of the three possible charges that could have been levied would have been a low grade (class C) felony – failure to affix tax stamps to the plants. If you grew marijuana in Kansas back in 1996, you had to affix to the plants "Kansas Department of Revenue stamps, labels or other indicia." How many? That depends on the weight of the plants, which, because they're in the ground, is unknowable.

But my wife and I were lucky. We walked. I was arrested but not charged. It was a first offense, so we got diversion. I did some writing and editing for Big Brothers/Big Sisters to fulfill my community service requirement.

Even though I wasn't charged, I was booked. After a lifetime of trying to prove to myself and others that I was Mr. Principled Nice Guy, it was startling to see my mug shot profile. The experience didn't lead just to a diversion but a conversion.

"Small time loser" isn't something I wanted on my vita. I had reached the final chapter of my book: *Getting Busted Is Shit.* My pot-growing days were over.

•

In an essay titled "Salvation," in her book *Amazing Grace,* Kathleen Norris describes a friend who has an awakening. The friend was in business with a man. One day, the friend and his partner "were driving on the outskirts of the small city that was to be the base of their operations," Norris writes, when "his friend veered, suddenly, onto the shoulder of the road. He had seen an acquaintance driving past in the other direction and was debating whether to turn his car around and follow him. 'I need to kill him,' he said matter-of-factly, reaching for a gun that our friend had not known was stashed under the front seat. 'I need to kill him, but he's with someone, and I don't know who. So it'll have to wait. Damn.'

"'It was right then that I decided to get out,' [our friend] said. 'This was over my head.' "

Reading this essay, I learned that the Hebrew word for salvation means, literally, "to make wide." Norris, alluding to this, writes, "Our friend had recognized that the road he had taken was not wide enough to sustain his life; it was sufficient only as a way leading to death." Though he had left that narrow road, he seemed, according to Norris' account, "a bit lost. He had tasted a kind of freedom and wasn't sure what to do about it, except to tell the story."

Stepping away from my relationship with marijuana, I, too, tasted freedom and experienced a widening of the road. For years, dope-growing seemed to me good, sneaky fun. It was a way to thumb my nose at convention, to pimp squares. Then, after the bust, it dawned on me that every spring for years, a portion of my consciousness and not a little of my emotional energy had been occupied with sprouting marijuana seeds in wet Kleenex, planting them in peat pots and, after they burst through the earth, hardening them off by setting them outdoors on chilly nights. This ritual, too, had become a kind of addiction. And all along the course of their young lives, I worried. Would the seeds sprout? (They'd been in my freezer for years.) Would the sprouts flourish once they were in the peat pots? Was I giving them too little water – is that why they wilted? Too much – would they spindle and rot?

Summers, I paid a tithe of worry about the plants being stolen, about their being seen by the meter readers from the utility companies. I worried, too, about explaining them to visiting parents or relatives. I was afraid to invite strangers to a party. Each fall's harvest was accompanied by fear and concealment. My refrigerator freezer was full of dope. My mother asked my brother, "Do you know why Roger keeps all that spinach in his freezer?" Poor mama. She must have suspected something, not to ask me.

The *Pot: Growing It* chapter got darker by the year, so gradually I hardly realized it. After the end, I realized how much freedom I'd sacrificed. Only when the rituals I'd engaged in for years were gone did I recognize their weight.

Another dimension of the loss of freedom was that, because of the illegality, I generally had to be silent about my elaborate engagement with the drug, except with friends.

•

It's odd. With marijuana, I started with *Toking: The First 30 Minutes* and loved it. *Pot: The Habit,* coming later, was cumulatively oppressive. With God I'm starting with a chapter titled *God: The Habit.* I pray, go to church, read and talk about God, pray some more – the habits of the religious quester. I'm hoping these behaviors eventually lead to a feeling for the divine. *Fake it till you make it* is one piece of recovery program wisdom that I buy. If I'm lucky, the last chapter of this book would be titled *God: The High.* But that may not be in the cards for me. I'll leave that to the fundamentalists and try to resign myself to my current vision of God. I remain among the tiny minority of Americans who perceive the deity to be profoundly unknowable.

In any case, I believe that a grail self exists and in the first stages of addiction, that's actually what I was going for – the peace found in the early minutes of getting high. I believe the grail self is somewhere along the wide road of salvation, not the narrow road of addiction, and in those moments when I feel the pulse of that self beating inside me, God may be a little closer.

3.

Love the One You're Without

Activation of [brain] areas involved in cocaine addiction may help explain the obsessive behaviors associated with rejection in love.

"Reward, Addiction, and Emotion Regulation Systems Associated with Rejection in Love"
Journal of Neurophysiology / July 2010

Romantic love has been called "a religion of two." Some fantasize that such love, when they find it, will be a cocoon inside which the unpleasant details of their character and those of the beloved will disappear. Typically, romance starts with a chance meeting; not long after, you get a special delivery telegram from Eros announcing that *You've won The One!* You phone friends halfway across the country, who, you later learn, chuckled to each other about your blathering.

Love's first blush arises from surges of an amphetamine-like chemical, phenylethylamine, or PEA, according to scientists, and it is the work of the limbic region of the brain, a structure much older, in evolutionary terms, than the cortex, the seat of reason. Carl Jung didn't have it quite right when he said that "the meeting of two personalities is like the contact of two chemical substances." The chemistry of these meetings is actually more complex, involving, besides PEA, serotonin (the chemical that today's antidepressants make available to nerve cells), opiates and oxytocin. Some of these serve other forms of love than romance (mothers nursing infants, for example, benefit from oxytocin) and some kick in at different stages: Mature, comfortable love, for example, is helped along by self-manufactured opiates – the same chemicals that account for the runner's high.

But more than chemistry figures into love. Learning is also crucial. Three psychiatrists, Thomas Lewis, Fari Amini and Richard Lannon, writing in *A General Theory of Love*, say that the qualities of character, personality and behavior in another that trigger romantic love are etched into our psyches. They call these qualities "Attractors," and they are the leavings of how we saw love played out before we knew the word for what we were seeing. The brand of love given us by mothers and fathers, sisters and brothers, aunts and uncles and nannies may be the kind we seek, again and again, as adults. And so we find partners who will genuinely love us, pick on us, abandon us, hit us . . . or vice-versa.

Context also shapes love. Obsessive love, for instance, thrives on hurdles. The higher they are, the more magnetic the attraction. Andreas Capellanus, aka Andy the Chaplain, who promulgated the rules of so-called "courtly love" in the 12th century, acknowledging the desire-whetting power of barriers, insisted that romantic love must needs be adulterous. Ethel Sector Person, in a book titled *Dreams of Love and Fateful Encounters*, writes, "Whenever a series of ongoing encounters between two people is structured in such a way as to foster intimacy within the context of a holding environment (one in which limits are set), love may be promoted." Having fallen hard for lesbians, married women and those too young for me, I understand the desire-whetting power of barriers to fulfillment. Big love launched me into various failed attempts at bonds in my youth. I'm sad to say that my "youth" lasted into my 40s or 50s, and I opened myself to love's irrational exuberance – and to emotional adultery – even after marrying. In the service of these "loves," common sense flew out the window.

Along the way, I learned that it's a good thing (for me) when there's time for romantic love to erode naturally, for it to be worn thin before it breaks. In that case, friendship is still possible. I'm friends with my first two wives, for whom I fell hard, because the "love" (by which I mean the romantic/idealizing kind) decayed slowly. But in other cases, when I wasn't prepared and love failed cataclysmically, the mourning lengthened and friendship became impossible. In those cases, the "religion of two" became a purgatory of one. The too-slender consolation of such losses is the lessons they teach. For this knucklehead, they became the way I learned to remain faithful to my current wife.

•

"Stealth love" is the most dangerous species I know. I am talking about women I knew and appreciated for years, but in a brotherly way. The woman might be struggling with, say, alcohol, a neglectful husband, a chronic illness or serial relationship failures. After years of therapy, I became a great listener, practicing, in effect, without a license. As I mentioned earlier, because of my eagerness to listen and advise those who struggle, my therapist took to calling me the "ambulance driver." When I gave counsel and support, some of that was reciprocated, of course, and gradually, tender feelings sprouted, of the grade-school-crush variety. I kept my affections a secret, both from myself and from their object, as they kindled, and, all the while, failed to notice (or refused to) that I was paying more attention to my sisterly "friend" than to my spouse.

During the courtship of my current wife, Barbara Yoder, I became infatuated with a married woman who was sharing more intimate conversation with me than with her husband. Once, at a session with Barbara, our therapist gave me a new job title. She turned to her and joked, "Being married to Roger is comparable to being married to a surgeon – only Roger doesn't make any money for his services."

As I mentioned in the previous chapter, my eagerness to listen and advise led me, years ago, to temporarily join a 12-step group, Codependents Anonymous. In the group I learned that codependents share an obsessive desire for love from people who, for one reason or another, can't give it. The codependent person depends on the other for his sense of self-worth and identity.

I suspect I learned to love the wounded by watching my mother tend to my broken father. Her seeming self-sacrifice, coupled with her patience in the face of his war-bred post-traumatic stress disorder, was alluring. Unfortunately, my soul was less pure than Mom's. She might give herself away, asking nothing, or little, in return, but I wanted something back from those I tended to. The problem was that by the time I blurted my feelings to the victims of my caretaking, I was drunk on them. When the woman, caught off guard by the disclosure, didn't reciprocate (and more likely felt slimed by my confession), my intensity, fueled by an awareness that I'd made a terrible mistake that would likely kill the relationship, ramped up, and things went from bad to worse.

•

The first time I experienced a relationship going off the tracks in the way I've described was almost 30 years ago. The near-term cause for the derailment? Seventeen words I spoke to a friend, whom I'll call Helen. At least that's what I told myself for a long time.

What really did us in, though, was the panic I felt about losing this friend and the obsession with getting her back in my life. The obsession made me a stranger to myself: Who was this person putting on *my* clothes, driving *my* car to *my* job? It also wrecked my marriage.

Until Helen, though I'd fallen in love, I'd never become fixated on a relationship. In fact this fixation prompted me to attend my first Codependents Anonymous meetings.

A mutual friend suggested it, so I calculated that this would please Helen and hasten a rapprochement between us. Wrong again. The hundreds of journal pages I filled between fall 1987 and 1990, when Helen and I attended a workshop together trying to repair the damage, won't let me forget how crazy I got. Reviewing those pages still leaves me baffled about my behavior.

•

Helen and I had met at the end of the 1970s. We were both writers. She was opinionated but reserved, even shy, when it came to critiquing my stories, yet there was an ease between us based on mutual respect. We were both intense characters, who shared an appetite for literature and had, to some extent, parallel pasts. We had both lived in communes and, around the time we met, were starting to think about getting straight – or straighter, anyway. We also both had had difficult relationships with our fathers.

Our friendship burgeoned. We shared a critical edge, a know-it-all cynicism. We were like bright kids who laugh and whisper conspiratorially about others' shortcomings. We had a sharp eye for their flaws and vanities, less awareness of our own. Our supervisors vexed us. We fumed and plotted and bad-mouthed them, experiencing the kind of high you get from feeling as if you're above the common lot. Having that kind of attitude can get you fired. Finally, I was – almost. I was lucky to be transferred out of the public relations office and into that of a vice chancellor who'd mentored me.

•

A few years after the transfer came the rift. Helen and I spent huge amounts of time together in those days. Our friendship began to expand beyond the work week, to include some weekends. Our partners were drawn in, too.

Slowly, I found myself attracted in a new way to her. One day I saw her hand resting on the table, the long fingers, delicate and tapered – a piano player's. Some awareness of her as a physical being precipitated in that moment, much as it might between a boy and a girl who'd been childhood friends but then came into sexual maturity. Meanwhile, outside my awareness, I gradually abandoned my wife. We had met as undergraduates, and now were turning 40. I didn't grasp the details of love's maintenance, as articulated by William Carlos Williams in his poem "The Ivy Crown": "Romance has no part in it./The business of love is/cruelty which, /by our wills,/we transform/to live together." Gradually, my dependency on Helen enlarged, fed by our frequent and intense contact and the taboos against a too-great intensity of feeling between male and female friends – especially between a married man and a woman.

Then things began to change. Part of the reason for my attraction may have been a dim awareness, around that time, that Helen was beginning to slip out of my life. I was still carousing on weekends, but Helen had quit. I didn't know this at first. She was probably anxious about sharing it. I had a secret about our relationship – my growing dependency on our emotional connection – and so did she – a need to distance from someone with habits she was leaving behind. Perhaps, sensing that, I panicked.

Because of the panic, I felt an urgency building: to say something to Helen about the tenderness I felt for her. So one day after lunch, I asked her to sit down for a moment outside the student union. She remained standing. But I sat down to steady myself to utter the words that I have never forgotten. They were the start of my downhill slide into an obsession that ultimately ended our friendship.

"You know, if we didn't both have partners I'd court you," I said. The "if" clause . . . the gentle word "court" . . . surely those protected me from the accusation that I was coming on to her.

She moved back a step, startled. I ignored the body language. I heard only her words: *Roger, that's so flattering.*

And then I heard my response: *Helen, I've loved you for years.*

I didn't realize it then, but the words were spoken in hopes that I would hear them seconded by Helen. The following week, feigning casualness, I asked her reaction to what I'd said.

You always seemed like a brother to me, she said.

My heart sank.

You know, I said, *in the future, I want to be more open about my feelings. Not like Woody Allen. Just a little more open.*

I was saying I had a right to say what I'd said. Defensively.

Then, Helen said something about *problems with men in the past*. I was hurt to be wound into a skein of troubling men.

After that lunch, I wrote an apology for having spoken so openly. Despite my drafting and redrafting the letter to get it just right, it was several pages long, and the length bore witness to an intensity that was all wrong. When we next met, she said she wanted time out from our friendship.

I'm afraid I've ruined everything.

No you haven't, she chided. *We've been friends for what . . .*

. . . eight years.

Eight years. It's just going to take time.

Ever eager to please (and without realizing that my statement was a ploy) I told Helen I had scheduled a session with a therapist she was seeing at the time.

•

In the months that followed came waves of journal entries and e-mails and notes to many of our mutual friends and my therapist as I sought to untangle the web I'd woven and to make sense of (and rationalize) my behavior.

It boiled down to this: Helen had regarded my words as a betrayal of the friendship; I felt wounded and angry about this; so we polarized. Helen and I had seconded each other for years, so her perception of my words cast doubt on mine. In her mind, I'd made a pass at her.

When I learned that Helen had said to a mutual friend, *He betrayed the friendship*, my psyche fibrillated. Part of me conceded that was true, while another part rose to my defense.

I wanted to see Helen's withdrawal from the relationship as her problem—as if she had fled because of my simple goodhearted sharing of honest feelings. I was so caught up in my suffering that I could not begin to empathize with what it was like for her to be the object of my relentless, intense focus.

Today, I recognize that my attraction to her was understandable, given our emotional intensity and daily contact. But why did I feel compelled – even pressured – to share my feelings? I don't know. The heart has its reasons, as Blaise Pascal said, of which reason knows nothing.

•

A healthy brain is like a city at night, with nerve cells firing at different times, their "lights" twinkling on and off. In an epileptic seizure, by contrast, there is a pulsing: a rhythmic firing of brain cells over large regions. That's how my brain felt when Helen suspended our friendship. I was convulsed by repetitious thoughts and feelings whose comings and goings I could not control. My mind's focus shrank. I reviewed, over and over, what had happened, faulting myself for insensitivity, then Helen for being thin-skinned.

I pondered what was said and what wasn't, what was implied and what wasn't. I was assured by her partner, who seemed remarkably calm through all of this, that I had only to be patient, that things simply needed time to heal. But I couldn't put the brakes on. To anyone who would listen, I talked compulsively about what had happened – defying Helen's request that I keep the matter between the two of us.

A therapist to whom I described all this wrote the following: "When the object of obsessive love asks for space, and the pursuit and intensity continues it feels like a profound violation. It's scary. The only safety is in ending the relationship, even if it's wrenching to do so. Every therapist will tell the object of obsessive love to take a 'no contact' position."

A Buddhist slogan says, "Of the two witnesses, trust the principal one." Pema Chodron, a Buddhist nun, writes in *Comfortable with Uncertainty*, "One kind of witness is everybody else giving you his or her feedback and opinions. This is worth listening to; there's some truth in what people say. The principal witness, however, is you." I continued to be caught between **my need** (for reconciliation) and **Helen's need** (for no contact). What made me crazy was my fluidity in moving between my judgment and Helen's – as if there were, in this case, **two** principal witnesses.

If that was what was happening at the level of reason, at the emotional level, something else had begun. I had entered what psychiatrist Stanislav Grof calls a "spiritual emergency": "An individual may suddenly feel a childlike sense of loneliness that seems completely inappropriate to his or her situation." I had many friends – I see their names as I page through my journals and letters from 1988 – but their love and attention provided no comfort. If all their love combined could have been put in one tray of a scale and Helen's rejection in the other, the Helen tray would far outweigh the other.

Mystified by this, I wanted to do more than understand my response. I wanted to solve the problem. With words. Words I imagined writing to Helen – and sometimes did write, in letters, some sent, most not. If I could just get five minutes with Helen, I thought . . . just explain what had happened . . . things could be right again. I wrote and wrote, seeking the words that would heal everything or at least explain it. But Helen requested I not contact her, and every word I sent to her pushed her farther away.

So I began to keep a journal. The entries from 1988 are as repetitious as those of a teenager's diary: the laser focus on longing, the melodrama of chance encounters with Helen. Once, we passed in our cars, driving in opposite directions. I waved. She didn't wave back. I'm embarrassed to confess that I went to her office to ask why. (She hadn't seen me.) Again and again, if there was a little healing, I tore off the scab.

My mistake was trying to will Helen's forgiveness, coupled with my failure to grasp just how much I had scared and offended her. At some level, I think I believed her forgiveness would redeem me. But redemption requires penitence, and penitence requires admission of responsibility and remorse. I could make no such admission. James Hillman, a Jungian psychologist, in an essay titled "Betrayal," writes, "Something comes out that has been held in . . . a confession, a poem, a love letter, a fantastic invention or scheme, a secret, a childhood dream or fear — which holds one's deepest values. At the moment of betrayal, these delicate and very sensitive seed pearls become merely grit, grains of dust. The love letter becomes silly, sentimental stuff, and the poem, the fear, the dream, the ambition all reduced to something ridiculous."

In the end, as Rosemary Sullivan writes in *Labyrinth of Desire*, "When obsessive passion is over and the projections are ripped away, the person standing there is almost always a stranger." That's what Helen became for me and I for her.

•

One day, I woke up crying. I stayed home sick that day, crying on and off. When my wife came home from work, I was still at it. I had never cried so long or mourned from such depths. She drove me to the therapist's office. When nothing else worked, the therapist and the masseuse officed next door had me lie down on the floor. Each took a leg, lifting it, flexing it, rocking it side to side the way you might a baby's. I wept from a place inside me that was utterly unfamiliar.

The climax of this phase was a night of hard praying in a hotel in Maryland. I was attending a conference of university editors. It was the first time since my undergraduate years that I'd prayed, and on this night it was for self-forgiveness and for relief from my own anger and despair. Finally, I stopped twisting the sheets and fell asleep.

Talking with friends (most of whom had kicked God to the curb long ago) about this experience, I'd minimize it. But in fact prayer dissolved my obsession and quieted my rage as nothing else had. I finally realized that getting

Helen back in my life wasn't the balm I needed. What I needed was to quiet my rage.

Whenever anger arose in the months after that – in the sauna, in the shower, in bed, walking down the street, reading a book, watching a movie, watering the lawn, talking with a friend, taking a shit – I prayed for its disappearance. I found comfort in the Lord's Prayer, the 23rd Psalm, the Jesus mantra — Lord have mercy, Christ have mercy, Lord have mercy.

Hillman helped me find other spiritual meanings locked inside this experience. He writes, "Just as trust has within it the seed of betrayal, so betrayal has within it the seed of forgiveness." My moral obligation in the situation became clear. Who had done what to whom was irrelevant. I had to forgive: myself, Helen, everyone. No exceptions. Nothing mattered so much as this fact: My rage was killing me, had always been killing me, just as it had almost killed my father, who'd had four heart attacks and then suffered congestive heart failure. Learning to quiet my heart was more important than *any* friendship. If it was God who delivered me from obsession, then in this case God was an asylum orderly who pried my fingers off the corpse of my affection for Helen.

An embryonic faith had split the shell of disbelief and wiggled out all hairless and dirty. I had become "conscious of myself as a spirit," in the words of Soren Kierkegaard. That gain, he said, is an infinite one, but it's "never attained except through despair."

•

Almost three years after all this began, Helen and I went to a weekend psychological workshop, hoping to patch together our friendship. There she told a dream in which she had a hand-held remote control with a freeze button on it. Any moment, an invisible alligator might materialize somewhere in space — perhaps with its jaws around her head — and she had to hit the freeze button fast. She said she saw me as the alligator. I was shocked — I had perceived *her* as holding all the power. The workshop facilitator suggested that when either of us felt engulfed by the other, we hit the freeze button and talk. During that workshop, something hard that had been stuck between us seemed to dissolve.

One evening, after we had witnessed a particularly emotional session involving a couple, we sat in chairs beside each other. She suddenly grabbed my hand. I was thrilled. Later, I drove her home. I turned off the engine and then we embraced for a long time. We each admitted having missed the other, especially our conversations.

The relief was immense, but we never fully recovered our trust.

•

When two people grow close, they make a third person, a composite of the two. In addition to loving each other, they love that third person, which they uniquely constitute. The old third had been smart, confident to the point of uppityness, and, at times, uncomfortably self-conscious. The new third was wary and watchful. Under its scrutiny, we lost our ability to play, our words became cautious. We hid from each other.

Helen set the terms of our new relationship, and we met just once a week, for lunch. This was smart, given that the frequency of our meetings earlier on had heightened the intensity of my feelings. But I didn't understand this then, and, desirous that our new relationship be a twin of the old one, I bridled. I thought about composing an oral history titled *Best Friends/Bitter Ends.* I would speak to parties on opposite sides of broken friendships, letting the silence between the two perspectives speak for itself. At lunch one day, feeling bitter, I shared the idea with Helen. Helen said she wanted to focus on the future, not the past. That was our last get-together. There was neither interrogation nor protest, only the unstated certainty that something had ended.

We never spoke to each other again.

•

On November 6, 1992, while driving alone at night on a dark road south of town, my chest opened. It was as if Helen's spirit had been lodged in my body and now decided to depart. I bawled and shouted, *I really did love you.*

In June 1993, six years after I told Helen I loved her, I had a dream.

Helen surprises me with a rewrite of one of my stories. I feel touched that she went to the bother, and I say that I will substitute her version for mine. She had never expected that, she says. She just wanted to show me another way to tell the story. I read it and realize, with regret, that mine is flawed. It has the distant tone of, say, a story about a science experiment. Her story is a fluid narrative. But as I mull hers, I see flaws in it, too. In the end, I decide to keep my version of the story, even with its flaws.

Years later, I sent Helen a letter, a photo of a turtle camouflaged among leaves and another of a snail ascending a stalk of horsetail, the lone survivor of a family of plants that has been around 300 million years. Here's part of what I said in the letter:

Your effect on me has been lasting. Besides the residue of memories – from playing Ms. Pac Man at the laundromat to our attempt to strike a truce at the workshop – the end of our friendship had a profound influence on the direction of my life.

As I worked to deal with my rage and my crazy behavior, something inside me shattered, something old and hard that had to shatter if I were to grow. My confrontation with rage was the most important work I ever have done, the beginning of a long process of conversion into someone softer than I had been.

•

I once got a rejection letter from the editor of a religious magazine, who said about my description of my inability to connect firmly with God, even after that night in Maryland, "I suggest that in your struggle, God is present to you; in your feeling of his absence, perhaps he is present." I knew what he meant. The absence of Helen from my life was, for months, one of the most powerful "presences" I have ever experienced. But it was not a comfort. If this is another of God's guises, it is not God the Father, the Son or the Holy Spirit. It is God the Question.

•

Today, my love has a single focus, my wife, Barbara Yoder.

Our love is not a religion of two. It is more mundane, the result of careful attention to detail, to taking notice of what needs doing and doing it or needs saying and saying it. It is a love that washes dishes and cleans the cat box, that frets about how hard Barbara sometimes tries to be good because it knows how draining that can be.

Psychologist William James wrote a little more than a hundred years ago of a "form of regeneration by relaxing, of letting go."

"It is but giving your little private convulsive self a rest," James writes in one of the Edinburgh lectures that appears in the *Varieties of Religious Experience: A Study in Human Nature*, "and finding that a greater Self is there."

Barbara and I both have rather more than our share of this "little private convulsive self." I try to give this fretful part of me more time off than I have in previous relationships, but I frequently do a lousy job. The love between Barbara and me is not untroubled. Things still go wrong. There are sinking spells. There is occasional drama, but nobody drowns.

Is there any good in the pain that chars you when an obsession has run its course? Any use in nights when you twist the sheets and days when the sun won't move? Sarah Miles, in the Graham Green novel *End of the Affair*, says: "I'm beginning to believe in you, God. And maybe that's how you work. You empty me of love and then fill that emptiness."

Indeed, the void left when love disappears may be a fertile space in which God can bloom, if you're graced.

Church of the Last Chance

I didn't feel much like a Christian and wondered if I was making a serious mistake. I longed to take refuge in Simone Weil's position, that her true religious calling was to remain outside the church. But that was not my way. I still felt like an outsider in the church and wondered if I always would.

Kathleen Norris
Amazing Grace

In the 1990s, one-third of the Americans who answered "yes" when asked if they "had a religious preference" nevertheless said that they attended religious services only once a year or less. Yet about half of the people who said they had no religious preference nevertheless said that they believed in God.

Michael Hout and Claude S. Fischer
University of California, Berkeley
From a paper delivered at the American Sociological Association/August 2001

4.

Knock-Knock

Ever since my first crush, on cute, blonde-haired Sharon Horton in the fourth grade, which, by force of will, I managed to conceal from everyone but my rival, a horrible boy named Amos, I have been a blurter when it comes to feeling attracted to someone. The last time I confessed such feelings, in a letter to a cute, blonde-haired woman friend in 1997, I believed, as usual, that this admission would make her day, or at least not be unwelcome. She was horrified. A mutual friend went to talk with her, trying to patch things up. She told him the whole thing had reminded her of some incident with a creepy guy who lived next door when she was 14.

Carrying the torch for Sharon made a lasting impression. Its residue was the feeling that the purest love is that which is felt but, because of circumstances, can't be expressed, or, if expressed, only because of powerful internal pressure and then, given that it's so freighted with need, is probably doomed. Love that lacked the tang of obsession and compulsion, in other words, was somehow less. I still believed this past age 50, though I had not articulated it to myself as clearly as I have here. Then I found a therapist who, after a few years, was able to pry this nugget of wisdom loose and reveal its essence: fool's gold. It makes me wonder what other nutty ideas I harbor about life's most crucial issues.

•

After my friend dumped me, I began to resort daily to the campus chapel to pray. The chapel had several advantages. It was small and unchurchy. It was always empty around lunchtime. No one I knew would see me there.

I hadn't stepped inside a church since high school, except on compulsory occasions, like the death of a relative, friend or acquaintance, or to please my mother on my infrequent visits home. In 1901, in a magazine called *The Monist*, James Henry Leuba, a psychologist of religion and Bryn Mawr professor, wrote that "God is not known, he is not understood; he is used – sometimes as meat-purveyor, sometimes as moral support, sometimes as friend, sometimes as an object of love."

I went to the chapel in order to use God, despite the fact that I could barely utter his name. (Once, in conversation with a friend, when I was unable to do this, she pounced, saying "you can use the 'G' word. It's OK.") "God" is such a tiny word – but dense as osmium, weighed down by associations, assumptions and meanings, crippled by misuse, division and violence. "God" and his "will" are so clear to some – so easy to know and to see – that I feel dispossessed of, and resentful toward, the God they would foist on the rest of us.

However embarrassed I may have been to hang out in public with "God," it didn't stop me from praying, even in the face of chuckles and winks from the Inner Heckler, my constant companion. One day in the chapel, the heckler was amused by a prayer and note I found tucked in a hymnal. It read, "May the sacred heart of Jesus Christ be praised, adored and loved now and forevermore; holy Mary, mother of God, pray for us; St. Jude, St. of the Impossible, pray for me now and grant me my request." The handwriting was carefully formed, the letters large and round. The letter "i" had been dotted with a precisely formed zero. The writer added: "Pray this prayer nine times a day for nine days and you'll get whatever you wish for!" I kept the note several weeks, and, in defiance of my heckler, prayed the prayer, hoping to leverage God into resuscitating the comatose friendship.

I was vulnerable to the notion of such leveraging. For example, as a hitchhiker in the late '60s and early '70s, I sometimes chanted the Buddhist mantra *Nam myoho renge kyo* hoping to summon rides. (I didn't know what the mantra meant, which is *I take refuge in [or submit to] the wonderful law of the Lotus flower sutra*; I'd gotten the idea from a note scribbled on the back of a highway sign that said it would get me rides.) But in praying to Saint Jude to give me my friend back, I was ignoring a body of wisdom I had encountered a few years earlier at Codependents Anonymous meetings: namely that relationship can turn addictive, that craven dependency on another is bad, bad, bad.

This time, neither St. Jude nor Buddha delivered. Eventually, I figured out that I'd lost my friend for good. Just another clue in a long trail that led to an awareness that God isn't Santa Claus, despite the frequent conflation of the two. Those who, like me, have felt dissed by God when a petition didn't work should heed Isaiah 30: 19-21: ". . . He will surely be gracious to you at the sound of your cry; when he hears it, he will answer you. And though the Lord give you the bread of adversity and the water of affliction, yet your Teacher will not hide himself any more, but your eyes shall see your Teacher. And your ears shall hear a word behind you, saying, 'This is the way, walk in it,' when you turn to the right or when you turn to the left." The message here is that general direction – or the occasional nudge – is what we may expect from God. He's no puppeteer.

•

Anyway, strolling to the chapel one day, I see this woman ahead of me, whom I think I recognize. A vague intent forms. *I should catch up to her*. The heat of the day and the distance to overtake her discourage this. I'm walking slowly. But she's slower still. I catch up to her at the place where the avenue bends; the chapel is right across the way. If I hadn't overtaken her there, I would have crossed the street while she continued on to the student union, where she was headed for lunch, and I probably wouldn't be going to a Mennonite church today. (Disbelieving that *Everything Happens for a Reason* doesn't rule out the possibility, albeit slight, of magic moments.)

I knew the woman. I'll call her Diane, which will spare us and our partners embarrassment. Like me, she was an editor. Unlike me, she was an embodiment of socially responsible hipness, a muckety-muck in the local health-food coop, a talented singer, a barn-dance caller. Diane's one of those women whose appeal transcends her good looks. She also exudes what I'd call a rectitude pheromone, the same kind given off by those fetching women who spoke straight and true in '50s cowboy movies.

"You going to lunch?" she asks.

"No," I say. "I'm going over there." I point to the chapel.

"You go there often?"

"These days, yes. Personal crisis."

I want to breeze past the topic, but then I pause. I ask, "Do you go to places like that, too?" "Church" was a word that, like "God," I didn't want to say out loud. The phrase "places like that" was distancing, the subtext clear: I don't really do *the church thing*. If Diane were cynical about religion, which is what I figured, what with her hipness vibe, then my use of the words "places like that" would show that I, too, knew church was uncool.

I mean, it wasn't really a *church*, just a tiny chapel – and empty. Besides, it wasn't Sunday, but noon on a weekday. I wasn't going to church to pray. I wanted a timeout for a . . . uh . . . *prayer opportunity*?

In truth, of course, my petitions to whomever-or-whatever-might-be-lurking-around were, in fact, fevered, and that was good. Approaching God on my belly, sweat beading on my forehead, is the best way. Praying in calm times I often lose my focus and fall asleep, as even religious professionals like monks are said to do. Plus, when I pray from a calm center, the Inner Heckler tends to show up and mock me. *Who you trying to fool, buddy?*

But Diane surprises me. She says yes, she does go to "places like that." I feel relieved, less medieval. I scramble for an excuse to contact her again. I ask, "Can you recommend a spiritual book for me to read?" This wasn't a totally bogus line, OK? I was actually reading spiritual books at the time. Diane suggests Dorothy Day's autobiography, *The Long Loneliness.*

(None of the local libraries had it, which gave me an excuse to call her to borrow a copy. I read it eagerly, glad to learn that Day, a do-gooder, had resisted Christianity for years. When I had finished, I handed the book back to Diane, post-it notes wagging out of the book's margins, a display of earnestness. And to create yet another excuse for contact, I lent her a copy of Anthony Bloom's *Beginning to Pray*.)

I ask what church she goes to.

"Peace Mennonite," she says.

I freeze. I try to control my voice: "The people with the buggies? The ones with the black hats?"

She says I'm thinking of the Amish, not the Mennonites.

The web here gets pretty tangled, so let me do a quick-and-dirty: The word "Anabaptist" is a label that includes, primarily, the Mennonites, Amish and Hutterites. There are several subspecies of Mennonite, ranging from more to less conservative, more to less worldly. The gemisch can be confusing even to insiders.

The Anabaptist movement began in the early 16th century in affirmation of a Christian faith that was voluntarily chosen (and in opposition to the baptism of infants, a practice of both Catholics and Protestants). The Anabaptists thought baptism should be reserved for adult believers, those who had some idea of what kind of faith they were plighting their troth to. This and other Anabaptist positions were offensive enough to those who wanted to impress gurgling infants into the ranks of their faith that they started torturing Anabaptists in order to get them thinking straight. Consider poor shoemaker Geleyn Corneliss. In 1572, he was suspended by his right thumb with a weight tied to his left foot. His captors burned his underarms with candles and then settled down to a card game. I'll spare you the rest, but "Geleyn, the shoemaker, was tortured most cruelly of all," concludes Thieleman J. Van Braght, in a compilation of horrors whose full title no one ever wished longer: *The Bloody Theater or Martyrs Mirror of the Defenseless Christians Who Baptized Only upon Confession of Faith, and Who Suffered and Died for the Testimony of Jesus, Their Saviour, from the Time of Christ to the Year A.D. 1660.*

Today, the Mennonites are the most worldly branch of Anabaptism, although, as I say, wide-ranging in their worldliness. And Mennonites are as prone to infighting and cross-congregational and cross-conference disputing as any other religious group. At the time, I knew none of this. All I knew was that Diane (a lapsed Catholic) promised that I (fallen away from the United Church of Christ) could come to Peace Mennonite Church without having to eschew the internal combustion engine or zippers (which the Amish, who prefer buggies and buttons, live without). She told me I was welcome to come to Peace any time, adding, "Sometimes, Sunday school is even more interesting than church." The next Sunday, I tried both.

Not long after that, I dreamed Diane and I were in love. In the dream, she farted loudly. C.G. Jung would have said, if I'd been his patient, that the dream was trying to knock her off the pedestal I'd put her on. By e-mail, I told her the dream and, of course, confessed the baby crush I had on her. Up to my old tricks again. She wrote back, primly, that her sole interest was in a relationship she had recently resumed with a high-school beau.

What good boundaries, I thought, enviously.

•

Dorothy Day was a find. In the *Long Loneliness*, she gives a spiritual explanation for the kind of yearning that leads to an unreasonable elevation of the importance of others. She writes: "People have so great a need to reverence, to worship, to adore; it is a psychological necessity of human nature that must be taken into account." Evolution may have its reasons for the amount of adoration we humans squander on each other – reproduction being the main one – but the fact that our friends chuckle among themselves about our condition when we fall in love should be a clue about the reality of such adoration. No, when it comes to other people, adoration doesn't make a whole lot of sense, unless you're looking to join a cult. With God, I'm told, it does.

But what is the relationship of human love to loving the divine? A Benedictine priest, Sebastian Moore, makes the case that human "love" may foreshadow the possibility of divine love. He writes that desire and attraction can shift "from the simple pull of the beautiful other, through the phases and hazards of a relationship, to the pull of the mystery itself, the subtle 'come on' of a power utterly beyond our mind's grasp but able to communicate with us through love."

"God is love," the scripture says, so maybe love can lead us to God; that seems to be Moore's reasoning. I wish I could second Moore about the "subtle 'come on'," but with me, God has not been flirtatious. He seems, instead, to me to have started our relationship with a knock-knock joke.

God whispers, "Knock, knock."
I say, "Who's there?"
No response.
"Who's THERE?"
No response.
"WHO'S THERE?!?"

Now Day, who seems more practical in her approach to God than Moore, says that "you love God if you want to love Him." If that's so, I have to set to work to raise my wanting quotient. This approach to God seems more promising to me than Moore's. My therapist has convinced me that love (for other humans) isn't so much found as made. It is made not only by being supportive of our partner, but by withholding our meanness.

Still, I recognize that Moore's position is more seductive and romantic. It is comforting to think God may have availed himself (or herself or itself?) to me within a woman's smiled invitation to come to her church. If God is the census-taker of the few hairs left on my graying head, then God surely would have known that this would be the perfect ruse to get a fool for love inside a church again. But the idea of God's arranging mini-dramas by the billions, 24/7, doesn't make it for me. I'm with William James, author of *Varieties of Religious Experience*, who wrote to Leuba in 1904: "I have no living sense of commerce with a God. I envy those who have, for I know that the addition of such a sense would help me greatly."

All this said, a shard of me desires to experience God as a safe bet, a sure thing, a certainty, a comfort, a divine Teddy Bear. A shard of me wants to get down with the snake-handlers. Do I contradict myself? Very well, then. If you think that the pursuit of God comes without contradiction, reversal and paradox, then you are a different brand of God-stalker than I.

I am the kind who waits for an answer to my *Who's there?* The kind Simone Weil, in *Waiting for God*, described: "The attitude that brings about salvation is not like any form of activity . . . . It is the waiting or attentive and faithful immobility that lasts indefinitely and cannot be shaken."

Since my chapel days, and my subsequent engagement with the Mennonites 18 years ago, this "faithful immobility," rather than unshakeable certainty, has been my way. A "living sense of commerce with God" would provide comfort, but it also might throw me together with Christians whose breathless certainty leaves me feeling a weird combination of longing, envy and scorn. I prefer those I've found at Peace Mennonite, who, like me, seem to doubt. Having breathing room matters to those of us who shrink from certainty, a word frequently paired, for good reason, with the word "dead."

5.

An Unlikely Mennonite

In our last chapter, you learned that I came to my first service at Peace Mennonite Church hoping that the acquaintance who'd invited me to come would eventually shuck her new beau. But she didn't. And so, a few months after coming to Peace, I started dating a woman born of Mennonites, from Goshen, Indiana, a Mennonite hotspot. (Pennsylvania, Ohio, Indiana and Kansas harbor more Mennonites than most other states.) Barbara and I married six years later, her father having expressed pleasure when he first heard my name. His hopes were (falsely) raised because "Martin" is a common Mennonite name.

But Barbara's not the reason I've hung in with the church – and more than hung in: Beginning as a back-row attendee who'd cut and run after service to avoid those falsely cheery, nerve-racking, post-worship conversations with strangers, I became an occasional reader of scripture, then a co-teacher of Sunday school for teens, then a member of the worship committee, several times. After a decade, I peaked, serving as church moderator – the lay leader. They even let me be on a pastoral search committee.

There wasn't any pushing or politicking required, given the size (small) of our membership. I tend to *make schput* (a phrase Barbara taught me, low German in origin, meaning to *mock*) about the church's some day purchasing a searchlight and using it to project onto the night sky a disc of light containing the silhouette of a dove, the Mennonite totem. Self-declaration and branding are as far from the Mennonite ethos as it gets. Plus, it would be a waste of electricity: In all the world, there are only a couple of million Mennonites. Those who attend Peace regularly number under 100 . . . actually, fewer than 70 . . . and, to be honest, on a busy morning we might hit threescore, 10 or 12 of them kids – though our pastor remains hopeful. There is, in short, no want of opportunities for service on any of what seem to be dozens of committees.

•

Returning to church relieved me of a guilt I'd felt toward my mother, a lifelong mainstream churchgoer of the pleasant and uncomplaining sort, one of those who doesn't have to make a peep for you to feel ashamed of somehow having fallen short. (When she lived in a rural setting southwest of St. Louis, even her inner circle of church friends lovingly labeled her a "goody-two-shoes" for never joining them in dumping on somebody during a gossip session.) When I stopped going to church, she let me know, but only occasionally, and then in an understated way, that she remained hopeful I'd return.

I'm sure my choosing a Mennonite flock surprised her. In the years after she moved to my town, she couldn't settle on a church and so called herself a Bapmethonite because she rotated among an American Baptist church, a Methodist church and ours. She would have preferred the local United Church of Christ but the place was too large and the acoustics – given her fading auditory powers – not the best.

When she came to Peace, I felt, sitting beside her, both pride for at last being the churchgoing son she hoped I'd become and self-conscious embarrassment that my "faith" is so pitiful, amounting to a dogged groping around inside the Big Dark of Unknowing. Her presence also made me notice when speakers and readers failed to use the microphone.

•

I've settled on the Mennonites because I find the views and ways of the small number of Mennonites I've met to be congenial. The emphasis on service to people living through a disaster or in disastrous circumstances is admirable. It's typical for young Mennonites to do a stint of voluntary service in communities where there are plenty of unfortunates, either chronically or temporarily. Then there's the emphasis on simple living, which, falling far short of the austerity of our Amish brethren, means that for Mennonites, someone's house may serve as a church. I've heard that Peace Mennonite Church grew out of volleyball games and the occasional keg, and that its first services were at a house.

Mennonites sometimes describe themselves as "countercultural," a term I find agreeable. They oppose the lashing together of church and state, for example, and in theory eschew politics altogether. Not all Mennonites share the same values to the same degree, of course. Most of those I know live in homes that fall well short of simplicity. They are just as cluttered as anybody's.

Even what is assumed to be a core belief of Mennonites – nonresistance – is nuanced differently, depending on which flavor of Mennonite you're talking about. (There are several, including "General Conference Mennonite," "Old Mennonite" and such. I've heard the names and acronyms – GC, OM, et cetera – drop casually from the lips of blood Mennonites, uttered with the ease and assurance of common understanding that a physicist might possess when she mentions muon or bosons.) Still, it's clear that our namesake, Menno Simons, a priest in Holland who converted to the faith, opposed bearing arms. He once asked, rhetorically, in a flourish of metaphors, "If Christ fights His enemies with the sword of His mouth, if He smites the earth with the rod of His mouth, and slays the wicked with the breath of his lips; and if we are to be conformed to His image, how can we, then, oppose our enemies with any other sword?"

Still, about half of the Mennonites drafted during World War II joined the military. And I recently heard about a Mennonite whose spouse, after his death, sold his gun collection for about $1 million.

•

I cannot guess what you might encounter if you decided to spend next Sunday at a Mennonite church. But if you came to Peace Mennonite Church in Lawrence, Kansas, you'd be likely to find a surprisingly high ratio of levity to gravity: lots of laughter and little sanctimony. Other places have more gravity. I once picked up a booklet in a Mennonite bakery in Oskaloosa, Kan., that faulted the deviation of today's Anabaptists from the ancestral path: "Most . . . have accepted or tolerated some or all of the following: fashionable attire, cosmetics, cut hair, jewelry, the unequal yolk with unbelievers in business and with false teachings in liberal, ecumenical religion, the radio and television (those sewer pipelines pouring the filth of the world into the home), the use of tobacco and strong drink, the participation in racial and national pride and prejudice, military service, fighting, killing, divorce and remarriage . . . and the play spirit."

Those who come to Peace seem unusually bright to me. That may be because we're in a university town. We are a brew of professors and teachers, editors and social workers, nonprofit-sector types and people with more concrete skills: builders, organic farmers, physical therapists. We dress down. I've lasted, to my surprise, through two blowups, the result of 1. divisions about welcoming gay men and women into our midst and 2. divisions about a pastor who was given a healthy shove toward the door by a vocal minority among us. Though that group didn't sack her, what happened was emotionally painful enough that eventually she left. So did many in the group who attacked her.

With that, tithes dwindled to a point that we couldn't afford a full-time pastor. Before the flight by many congregants, the church was always in danger of a drift toward heterodoxy, New Age-ism, nature worship and such. As we contracted, we became poorer and more conventional. We went from a full-time pastor, to a three-quarters time and then a half-time pastor. In recent years, we've gained a bit of traction; the pastor's position is now .6 time. We're also more decidedly Christian.

•

When I came to Peace Mennonite in 1997, it shared an important feature with Bethel Evangelical and Reformed Church, where I'd gone from birth till I entered the university in 1964. Both lacked air-conditioning. This seemed proper. Christians ought to be ready to endure a trickle – or flood – of sweat. In summer, Bethel buzzed with fans, but at Peace, the heat was oppressive, magnified by the worship space we were then renting: the second story of an ecumenical ministries building a block from the university campus, torrents of sunlight falling through the floor-to-ceiling windows and just a couple of lousy fans.

The sermon on my first day back at church after decades away sounded a lot like the sermons of my childhood, so I did the usual thing: spaced out. Perhaps sermons are doomed by the fact that a pastor must compose so many in the course of a career and that they must be written no matter the weather in the pastor's heart or the preoccupations of her mind. But I think at bottom my objection to sermons is structural. Their composition seems patchworky, their leaps less logical than associative.

In defense of those who preach – I've tried my hand, too – the abstractness of spiritual topics lends itself well to incoherence. Words and sentences often clang, or worse, against the mysteries they seek to describe, making sermons, in my experience, as difficult to remember as dreams. Spare expression coupled with silence may be best when talking about God and his son, powers and principalities, good and evil – but sermons tend to move in the opposite direction.

•

Besides the likenesses between Peace and Bethel, there were several notable differences. Bethel had certain creedal staples: the singing of the Doxology, the recitation of the Apostle's Creed and the Lord's Prayer, for example. The Mennonite church is, in general, creed-lite. It's nice not having to mumble doctrines I don't necessarily assent to, or understand, until repetition has dulled their meaning and bled them of feeling. In the old days, even when the Lord's Prayer made its way into services at Peace Mennonite, it wasn't the conventional one. We read the New Zealand version, with its references to *eternal spirit* and *earth maker* and a genderless *father and mother of us all.* Eventually, I began to yearn for "daily bread" and wish for deliverance from evil, and others, too, must have felt that. The old prayer was restored to our liturgy after the congregational wars of the early 2000s.

The treatment of children has changed radically since I went to Bethel. Back then, there was no part of the service specifically for kids. In the 1950s, as during most of American history, children were regarded as adults-in-training; job No. 1 was to be seen and not heard, or, if heard, only in a timid and tentative voice, usually with questions related to urgent bodily functions. At Peace, as at many churches today, a fraction of the adult service is tithed to children. Most of the kids are then whisked off to their own room, in part to shelter the adults from their distracting outcries and in part to shield the children from bewilderment, boredom, shushings or glances. (Such signs of disapproval have resulted in the withdrawal or exit of families from Peace.)

One of the most obvious contrasts between my childhood church and the former site of Peace Mennonite is physical. Bethel, at the corner of Greer and Garrison streets in North St. Louis, was a ponderous granite structure, a mighty fortress that probably could have remained standing even if a nuke hit Cahokia Mounds, across the Mississippi in Illinois. Bethel had the conventional appointments: a pulpit elevated well above pew level, a pipe organ behind and above that, and, across from those, a small balcony. There were stained-glass windows and mahogany pews that the low notes of the organ caused to vibrate.

In the old days, Peace Mennonite had an upright piano, usually out of tune, especially in the warm months, and, on many mornings, flute or cello or guitar or banjo solos to start things. We sat in plastic chairs, not pews, staring out of plate glass, not stained glass. The first day, staring out those windows, I watched sycamores buffeted by a hot Kansas wind. I thought about the contrast with Bethel, where stained glass dampened the light that fell onto the funereal pews.

As an institution, Bethel Evangelical and Reformed Church had German and Swiss roots and was politically conservative, at least until the Evangelical and Reformed Church joined the denominational grab-bag known as the United Church of Christ in 1957. Some Mennonites, including Barbara, have Swiss roots, too. Yet the Peace Mennonite congregants that first day were starkly different from the women and men of Bethel. Their casual dress . . . the intellectual tone . . . the liberal politics – all this was more comfortable to me as a grown man than were the men in three-piece suits and fat cigars I encountered in church as a boy. In time, of course, I found that folks at Peace could be just as rigid as those at Bethel. Proud to be contrary, they strutted their heterodoxy. One of our more orthodox members called Peace the *Church of Anything Goes*, another the *Church of the Last Chance*. We had a reputation among other Mennonite churches in the region for our flakiness. For me, the fit was good

•

One of the features of Sunday services I found most appealing would never have happened at Bethel. A time for "sharing" was set aside after the sermon for people to reflect about it or to share their joys and sorrows or to ask for prayers. On my first Sunday back, a guest speaker had talked about victim-offender reconciliation. During sharing, a woman sitting next to me rose to say that she was "struggling" with the speaker's theme. Her voice broke as she asked for our prayers. It was the fourth anniversary of her divorce, she said. As she had been driving to church that morning, she was shocked to see her new boyfriend's car outside of his old girlfriend's apartment. *What courage to speak so openly*, I thought. (It wasn't till much later that my Inner Heckler popped this question: *Hmmm, how'd she happen to drive by the old girlfriend's apartment, anyway?*) At that moment I felt something I'd never experienced in a church: the pulse of the real. Her words were startling, the subtext clear and authentic: *I don't feel like reconciling this morning, I'm mad as hell at my boyfriend – or maybe EX-boyfriend.*

When the service ended, I turned to the woman and complimented her openness. "Peace Mennonite is the kind of place that allows you to be real," she said. This was my first conversation with Barbara. It's been 19 years since then, and, although the rough places haven't been made entirely smooth, we are happily married, me for the third time, she for the second.

For a number of reasons, this kind of sharing couldn't have happened at Bethel. That was the 1950s, when bad things happened only to bad people (or, if to good people, they were kept under wraps). Moreover, the Rev. Oscar Nussman was generally the only speaker at Bethel on a given Sunday, reading scripture; mining the Good Book for ore that, with considerable refinement and processing, could be turned into gold; telling people what page to turn to in the hymnal. The notion that others would speak was alien; the congregation should be seen but not heard, except en masse, during song or creedal recitation.

Some no doubt will think that sharing of the sort Barbara did is more fit for a 12-step program than a sanctuary, but as a blurter myself, I was touched. Had I felt encouraged by Nussman to be forthcoming as an adolescent, I might have said, *I'm just not getting Christianity, OK? I feel nothing when I eat the wafer and drink the grape juice. Just what AM I supposed to feel, anyway? I can't be the only one who doesn't get this. And BTW, in the bigger picture, with the world so broken, why doesn't the church seem to be part of the solution?*

I felt the *pulse of the real* my first Sunday at Peace Mennonite, and a possibility dawned: A church might admit – even invite – all of our humanity. Of course it may be, as my grandmother warned, that *there's a time and a place for everything* (meaning *not now and not here*). And perhaps calling for transparency, at church or anywhere else, is like Holden Caulfield's loathing all the phoniness around him:

puerile. In fact, Barbara admitted to me later that when she shared such things at Peace Mennonite as she had shared that morning, she often felt embarrassed afterward. Other people did not tend to be so deeply personal.

But a thought persists: Maybe a church can be more than a group that gathers in a ritual space once a week and occasionally, in between, for potlucks. After all, if we aren't transparent with our fellow congregants, what's to distinguish church from any other polite gathering?

•

Beyond the occasional authenticity, I find the political structure of our church pleasing. On the whole, Mennonites care less for hierarchy or centralized authority than most other Christian groups. Congregations may override conference authority. There is respect for the individual and small group, using the words and deeds of Christ, joined with the compass of conscience, to navigate through life.

I've said how easy it was for me to rise to a place of importance in our small congregation. Another way of saying the same thing is that everyone's contribution is crucial. Small as we are, if we don't all pitch in, we won't make it. But the importance of every person goes beyond need; it is also a function of the respect accorded to individual conscience. John Roth, an influential Mennonite thinker, writes in his book *Beliefs* that "Mennonites have generally assumed that the Bible is best interpreted in local settings" and that "study, reflection, discernment and action are expected from every member."

The respect for individual conscience means that Mennonites – or those I know, anyway – don't evangelize or press. They don't expect you to be slain in the spirit, to speak in tongues, to capitulate to a passel of strange doctrines. Laws are for powers and principalities, for states and cities. Laws are part of the secular city, not the holy city. Mennonites, while not rabidly anti-government, clearly answer to other authorities.

And Mennonites don't judge your place on the path to God (with some exceptions of course, including Mennonites who can't abide bed courtship or the play spirit). Except in traditional or rural Mennonite settings, the church doesn't seem to stand guard between the individual and Christ's way, as revealed in word and deed. On the other hand, the work of interpretation isn't undertaken alone. Mennonites speak of a "priesthood of all believers." C. Arnold Snyder, in the Epilogue to *Anabaptist History and Theology: An Introduction*, writes that "all human beings stand equally before God. So said the early Anabaptists, and they were right."

•

It's not that a church is going to be easy – ever, at least for me. When people do get real, pain may follow. And despite what I've said about the virtues of authentic sharing, people drift through the church from time to time who share a little *too* eagerly and provide too much information, ultimately raising doubts about the reliability of their narrative. And then the whispers start. In short, wherever religious people gather, difficult people (or even nut jobs) *will* show up. My mother put it discreetly: *They go to church, honey, because they're NOT perfect.*

Sometimes people go away in a huff. A Mennonite joke tells it all:

> *A group of rescuers comes to a small island where a bunch of Mennonites are shipwrecked. There are three structures on the island, so the rescuers ask the Mennonite about them.*
>
> *"Well this one over here," he says, pointing to smallest of the three, "is my house."*
>
> *Pointing to a second: "And that's my church."*
>
> *Then, pointing to the third, he says: "And that's the church I used to go to."*

When I came to Peace, I was hopeful that maybe it would live up to my fantasies of church. I fell in love at first sight, but then it turned out to be like most romances: The varnish peels off and you get down to the work of loving within the usual messy relationship. And part of the messiness is trying to love yourself when ***you*** fail to live up to the ideals of the place.

You might think that at the Church of the Last Chance there'd be forgiveness all around all the time, with everyone recognizing the truth of what theologian Walter Brueggemann writes in *Cadences of Home: Preaching among Exiles*: "Whereas the empire needs certitude, exiles need space, room for maneuver, breathing opportunities that allow for negotiation, adjudication, ambiguity, and playfulness."

Exiles may, indeed, need all that, but, sometimes, their personal history and sense of being outsiders make them brittle. Wherever 5 or 10 or 12 or 50 gather together for any length of time, whether in Birkenstocks or suits, alliances form, in-groups and out-groups spring up and people get hurt. As the crucible of community heats up, people may not open their hearts but close them. They may not allow their fellow exiles "room for maneuver" when an issue is hot and the vote is tight.

Peace Mennonite felt right to me when I came to it because as I listened to Barbara, it seemed to me a place where one's heart could be safely opened. Though we are right now in a peaceable passage, I'm wary.

We have seen our share of hard times.

6.

Sunday School at the Church of the Last Chance

The Sunday school . . . was an institution without which the church of Jesus Christ could get along for almost 1,800 years. . . .

Martin E. Marty
Christian Century

As a child, I liked Sunday school. Not all those in my generation shared the sentiment. An article appeared in *Life* magazine on Feb. 11, 1957, written by a Baptist minister named Wesley Shrader. Shrader speaks of a "Tom" who, at 14, came home and reported to his parents that Sunday school was "the most wasted hour in the week." For me, the Sunday morning church service was much more torturous.

One of the positives about Sunday school was that kids outnumbered adults. Another was the mode: informal Q & A. This was more pleasing than having to sit in a pew that was hard as a bone, listening passively to words that were neither interesting nor comprehensible – with some of them repeated every Sunday. There was a stage when I ran wildly about during some part of Sunday school. Yet on balance, the experience was good, so that, as an adolescent, I agreed to attend weekly Sunday school classes even after

I'd bargained my mother down on the number of Sundays I had to attend church.

Adolescence improved the experience of Sunday-school-like activities. I was 13 during my confirmation class year, when I learned to rattle off the names of the books of the Bible without pause, as if I were pronouncing one long word that began "Genesisexodusleviticusnumbers" and terminated with a series of baffling Johns and Peters before the final Revelation. Moreover, after being confirmed, at a dance party in somebody's basement, I reveled in the charge of libidinous energy and prepubescent longing that suddenly manifested. (Was it Nancy Bland's house? I remember dancing with tall, willowy Nancy.)

Then came Young People's League, a sort of Sunday-school-gone-wild experience. It, too, carried a sexual charge, which was enhanced by the prim restraint of our bunch as we did the usual things, the canoeing, the sledding, the caroling. The group was led by acne-scarred Nylin and his fiancée, Joyce, who were pretty young themselves. Their nuzzling, cooing and whispering fed the ambient, chaotic sexuality emerging in our group.

•

When I came to Peace Mennonite Church in June 1997, my first moments were spent in Sunday school. This is ironic. Historically, Mennonites resisted the institution. Sunday schools appeared in American Protestant church starting in the late 1700s, the invention of Robert Raikes who had "broad humanitarian interests in mind as he began to stir up support for educating the early victims of the industrial revolution," according to church historian Martin E. Marty.

But the first Mennonite Sunday schools didn't appear until the 1860s. They met "considerable opposition from their beginnings through the 1870s in every Mennonite community," writes Fred Kniss, in *Disquiet in the Land: Cultural Conflict in American Mennonite Communities*. In 1870, for example, anti-Sunday school laymen in Virginia compiled a list of 25 reasons why Mennonites in Virginia should abolish Sunday school. "Because it is something new," writes Kniss, was reason 12. But reason No. 7 was the most telling: "Because by the use of [Sunday school] we follow after something held in the highest [regard] by the world at large." The bias against worldliness could not have been helped by the fact that "worldly" Protestants and Catholics had murdered many a Mennonite in the 16th century. An aversion to a Protestant invention is understandable.

Then came John Funk. According to Kniss, in the 1860s, Funk organized Mennonite Sunday schools among the urban poor. He owned a publishing firm and used his magazine, the *Herald of Truth*, to promote Sunday school among Mennonites. At the time, most Mennonite churches convened only every other week. Mennonite youth were being lost to "more exciting programs in other denominations," Kniss writes. Sunday school was a way of using the church building on off-Sundays and "protecting young people from the influence of other denominations."

By contrast, at Peace Mennonite Sunday school, all sorts of spiritual threads got tangled up. Some who attended liked a splash of Buddhism with their Christianity; other preferred the reverse. This gave Rod, our pastor at the time, who'd grown up Pentecostal, fits. In his pleasantly modest way, he struggled to keep the weed of heterodoxy from growing too robustly. The drift toward ecumenism in Sunday school also ruffled the feathers of some of the ethnic Mennonites, including my wife, Barbara. In those days, she often felt like an outsider at Peace Mennonite. Of course a congregation in a university town like ours is bound to attract spiritual hoboes. (I washed up at Peace, after all.) And the non-conformist spirit of Mennonitism – emphasizing simplicity rather than materialism, peace rather than violence – raised the probability that non-conformists would be drawn to Peace Mennonite.

•

One summer, Rod took a sabbatical. The adult Sunday school class tackled those biblical books that, as Rod would have said, ministers don't care to preach from. These are the books that aren't quite on message. One Sunday, for instance, we examined the finale of Job, in which God, eloquent and in high rage, instructs Job to look at His creation and feel the proper respect. God points to something big and fierce – a "crocodile" in one translation, the "Monster of Chaos" in another – and says: "Who can open the doors of his face? Round about his teeth is terror. . . . His sneezings flash forth light, and his eyes are like the eyelids of the dawn. Out of his mouth go flaming torches; sparks of fire leap forth. Out of his nostrils comes forth smoke, as from a boiling pot and burning rushes. . . . Though the sword reaches him, it does not avail; nor the spear, the dart, or the javelin. He counts iron as straw, and bronze as rotten wood." Job is dazed. It's bloodcurdling stuff of the kind you'll also find, say, in Deuteronomy 28, where God sets forth a horrible string of curses that will be visited on the disobedient.

As we finished Job that Sunday, the group was asked what it wanted to address next.

"Let's bite on the big end of the stick," I suggested. "Let's do Ecclesiastes."

That's the book with the famous lines that contributed to the Byrds hit "Turn, Turn, Turn": *There is a time to be born and a time to die, a time to weep and a time to laugh.* King Solomon is said to be the source of the book. Its perspective is dark and reductive, its vision of life one of suffering. Indeed, says the book, men and beasts "all go to one place; all are from the dust, and all turn to dust again." The late William S. Burroughs, author of *Naked Lunch* and not a particularly cheery man, once told a mutual friend that Ecclesiastes was his favorite book of the Bible.

•

Then one day my phone rang.

"Will you lead adult Sunday school?" a voice asked.

Uh-oh, I thought. *Me? For Chrissake, what've I gotten myself into here? ME? What's wrong with these people?*

"Well, I really feel inadequate. I'm so newly returned to church. I mean, I don't . . ."

"You'll be great."

"Uh . . . OK."

I selected a few chapters and verses from Ecclesiastes that would provide ample gloom. In Chapter 7, for instance, the narrator says that "it is better to go to the house of mourning than to go to the house of feasting" and that "sorrow is better than laughter" and that "the heart of fools is in the house of mirth." Chapter 9 tells us not to expect to win the race just because we're fast, or to get rich because we've got brains; "time and chance" happen to us all. It's easy to see why Ishmael, the lone survivor of Captain Ahab's ill-fated voyage, called Ecclesiastes the "fine hammered steel of woe."

•

Back then, adult Sunday school was held in a giant public room within a building close to campus. We shared space in the Ecumenical Christian Ministries building with a few other religious organizations that wanted a near-campus presence. The space was furnished with a soiled braided rug, a sofa and a few plastic chairs arranged in a circle. When I arrived that day, I saw, to my distress, that every seat was filled.

A few regulars were on hand. Among them was Natalya, who had a mullet cut. One Sunday morning during a time dedicated to sharing, she told the congregation that in 7th grade she'd been circled by girl classmates and taunted, a perfect trauma for the forging of a Mennonite soul. John, then her husband, bearded, eloquent, nasal, with a fanny pack and an endearing stammer, came with her most Sundays. Together, they ran a small farm inside the city limits, inviting people to come pet the lambs one time of year and pick produce another. Then, John and Natalya divorced, and John left the church. Eventually, when the church decided to buy a small building formerly owned by the Odd Fellows, Natalya objected and left, too.

There was Merilee, who wore a different hat every Sunday morning and sang gospel beautifully and, for her day job, rehabilitated sex offenders. One year she became a member, but then met somebody, moved to Kansas City and quit.

There was Doug, with bouncy red curls and an intensity amplified somehow by his rail thinness and with him Shirley, his placid spouse. Doug seemed tickled to meet me, saying he'd heard my commentaries on Kansas Public Radio and enjoyed them. I was flattered, and we took to each other right away. I could get manic with him, and we sometimes giggled together in a way that made us both feel like goofy adolescents.

Eventually, both Doug and Shirley dropped out. Some time later I heard that Doug had started a cosmology discussion group to explore the spiritual implications of what physicists were finding out about the universe.

Four older people were visiting the day I led adult Sunday school. That unnerved me. If I'd known one of the four was a retired priest, it would have been worse. Here I was, coming in from a Fimbulwinter of faithlessness to be Sunday School Teacher for a Day. The presence of guests underscored my fraudulence.

•

Teaching Sunday school forced me to take an unnatural step: I felt compelled to put a positive spin on Ecclesiastes. Now I'm not Mr. Upbeat and neither was the narrator of Ecclesiastes. People sometimes tell me they have heard me laughing when they're out at a movie. My laugh is distinctive. It amazes me to listen to a tape I've made while interviewing someone. I'll hear this abrupt and raucous laughter – it sounds sort of whacked, as if it were escaping, like steam, under pressure – and wonder *Why is this man laughing?* It emanates, often, from a sense of life's ironies rather than from joy. It is hard for me to believe that there are honest options other than pessimism when it comes to our species. My father was not a man of ideas, but he did have one: that the wise person never trusts in life's continuity and is always braced for a sucker punch. It's a very Ecclesiastes thing to think.

Nevertheless, the day I led adult Sunday school, I made myself scour Ecclesiastes for upbeat notes. This is what I'd come to church for, right – a more hopeful mind? I owed the class this, because I presumed those who'd come were present for the same reason. I began by asking their impressions about the narrator of Ecclesiastes.

Doug said, "Well, he seems like a young man."

"My impression, too," I said. "He gives thumbs up to the pleasures of eating and drinking and working, but he's also inconsistent about that. For example, after he talks about the joys of labor, he later says that toil profits no one because we all die, eventually. His mind runs all over the place, like a young person's."

Thinking of Ecclesiastes as the blues song of a younger man makes the book less threatening.

"Does anybody see any rays of hope?" I asked.

Natalya offered this: "There's the passage about a handful of quietness being better than two hands full of toil and a striving after wind."

"Right! Good."

She continued: "And there's the statement that it's good to have someone else in your life, that two are better than one because with two, one can help the other if he falls down, but if you're alone and fall, you've got no one to help you up."

"That's right," I said. I felt a need to signal, somehow, that I'd done my reading. "There's the simple affirmation of the senses, too, isn't there? The line in Chapter 11, 'Light is sweet, and it is pleasant for the eyes to behold the sun.'" I remember someone's once saying, after a romance had ended, that he knew he was healing the day that he noticed a sensual detail in the world: Some letters on a building he had been walking into every day suddenly zoomed out at him – they were three-dimensional again. Even the poorest folk share in the wealth that are sunlight and sky; the just and the unjust both profit from rain.

Someone in the class pointed out that Ecclesiastes advises Christians to look to the hereafter for solace, citing these lines: "Fear God, and keep his commandments; for this is the whole duty of man. For God will bring every deed into judgment with every secret thing, whether good or evil." There's a hint, the person said, of a sweet hereafter for the soul who keeps a contract with God.

I don't buy the idea of going to my heavenly home, but it didn't matter. I thought, *Hey they're saying the right things!* and felt a glow. All teachers cherish the moments when students seem to be getting it on their own, and they all seem to want to talk. There's an eerie kind of elevation, a feeling that all the minds in the room are attuned to a common source. That's what happened during the first adult Sunday school class I'd ever taught. I didn't take this personally; I credit Ecclesiastes despite its gloom.

I had brought a handout, a photocopy of Chapter 96 of Herman Melville's *Moby-Dick*, where Ishmael, elaborating on Ecclesiastes, warns, "There is a wisdom that is woe; but there is a woe that is madness." I said, "The narrator of Ecclesiastes is almost crazy with despair, the deadliest of the seven deadly sins." (I've since found out that pride is the deadliest sin. The priest who came to class that day and who obviously knew this, didn't call me on it. *Poor kid, let him go,* he must have thought.) I asked the class what could be done with such despair. How could it be mitigated or transformed? Eventually, I passed around a handout that contained several prayers of Brother Lawrence, a cook, 17th century Catholic mystic and author of *The Practice of the Presence of God*. I pointed to a prayer that reads, "God, I submit to these troubles as long as you please, for I know that they will advance my devotion to you."

"In times when we suffer," I said, "God can seem really near." On the other hand, when things are good, it's easy to forget God. I read aloud a passage from Richard Wright's autobiography, *Black Boy*, in which he writes that the most meaningful times of his life were those when he had struggled to make meaning out of what appeared to be meaningless suffering.

"Amen," someone said.

The hour sped by, and I was sorry when time was up. John, the father of one of our members and a retired minister, complimented the class for having the courage to live with an awareness of paradoxes. He compared us to another Sunday school class he sometimes attends, whose members seek more definition and certainty, he said, along with a firmer image of God. I wanted to stand up, throw confetti and cheer. It seemed that a new way into the church had opened for me, a way to enter its collective life more fully. I felt a click – the kind I felt my first day at Peace, when Barbara rose and bore witness to her heartache.

It was just a click, not a turning point. The next week I skipped Sunday school – better keep my distance, play it safe. The pessimist knows that all things novel are pleasant in part because they ARE novel and that every time you try to repeat a pleasure, the pleasure decays a little. So I wrote off the afterglow of the class as beginner's luck. Even so, when I returned to Sunday school two weeks after my teaching debut, I felt a little pride hearing that the discussion of Ecclesiastes had continued in my absence – as if maybe I'd started something that had gained momentum.

I asked Merilee, the hat lover, "How'd it go? What did you discuss?"

"Chakras," she laughed.

•

If teaching adult Sunday school was a pleasant surprise, teaching the 8th to 12th grade set was a shock. But if you live long enough, you do plenty of things that seem improbable beforehand and inevitable after. Today, the fact that I fell in with Mennonite teenagers makes sense.

There was a hole in my life that needed filling. Rather than have children, my first wife and I had abortions, one in 1969, another in 1974. I know *I* was far too immature and temperamental to have raised a child properly. My wife and I imagined ourselves cultural outsiders – though I had only pretensions about being a writer, while she practiced her craft ever day. How would we be able to paint and write with a child making demands?

Moreover, I've never overcome my ambivalence about kids. Early on, feelings of terror prevailed. The times in my life when I've actually held an infant (fewer than the fingers on one hand), I've feared dropping or crushing it or, more likely, making it wail. Though the absence of a child from my life may have been the right thing, my life is theoretically more sterile for that absence. It's as if I've missed out on something as primal as sleep or sex. I tell myself I'm glad I didn't have to change diapers or butt heads with a 2-year-old, but I know that it's different when you're a parent. From a distance, I'm fascinated with the I-don't-give-a-damn-what-you-think-about-this spirit of a child, but annoyed, too, and exhausted by the relentless explorations. It's a miracle that so many adventurous and curious children turn into so many unadventurous and uncurious adults.

Being around children takes energy and vigilance. I feel compelled to meet a child's energy in equal measure, feel that being reserved around children is boring and German and what I never wanted to be on the receiving end of, so why should I stiff a kid with that? Friends tell me you get used to the vigilance that children require. Usually, those friends are chasing a kiddo as they tell me this, or snatching him up just before he launches into heavy traffic. I'm glad that my friends have had children because, in small helpings, I love kids. Theirs. I used to be bugged by most everything in the natural world, including babies and cats, but I've grown. Being a Sunday school teacher of teenagers pushed me beyond detached admiration and into something squishier that I thought I'd never feel.

•

Now I was never THE teacher. I was only assistant coach for a couple of years to the main guy, a humble, soft-spoken, bearded, 50ish Christian psychologist (and cradle

Mennonite) named Steve Unruh. He'd been teaching the class about seven years when I joined him.

When Robert Raikes reportedly inaugurated a Sunday school for the children of chimney sweeps in 1780, his purpose was to provide some reading skills to working-class children during the Industrial Revolution. Sunday school really was SCHOOL, as in learning to read – the Gospels, of course. By the time Steve and I got around to teaching Sunday school, more than two centuries later, it involved (at least for me) equipping the kids for spiritual mud-wrestling in the pits of doubt. I sensed that Steve wanted to be around at that moment in kids' lives when this idea began to wilt: that Jesus and his death on the cross mattered, that his sacrifice was our salvation. Steve wanted to be a rock in whatever storms might blow our kids away from this brand of faith. My reasons for signing on to help him were more anthropological. I wanted to be near a band of Earth's primo primates as they moved through the shocks of adolescence. I was also drawn to this age group for a less conscious reason: My teens were the last time I'd had a positive sense of organized religion.

The first three years I went to Peace Mennonite, Steve would stand up in church every summer and quietly ask whether another adult might want to teach the class in his stead. I imagined people bowing their heads and gazing fiercely at the floor; I didn't actually know because I was also hanging my head.

Then, one year, I said I'd help.

Besides pitying Steve, and beside my curiosity about the kids, I took the job because I figured it would fulfill my service obligation as a Mennonite. Performing this duty would save me from nailing my thumb to the sheetrock on some Habitat for Humanity project.

My first Sunday on the job I noticed that Steve cut the kids incredible slack. I wanted to get right to the lesson, but he'd start with a how'd-your-week-go query while the kids raided a box of Dunkin' Donuts that we provided. At my first check-in, the littlest kid, Scott, reported he'd broken

100 for 18 holes. The biggest kid – a towering 13-year-old named Ryan – talked about being cast in four separate roles in a community theater production of "Inherit the Wind."

For the next two years, I drank in the experience of the kids most every Sunday. I found I loved it even at those hard moments when they fell silent. The silence of teenagers is anything but quiet, or quieting. Certain glances were as loud as bombs exploding, even if I didn't know what the explosions meant. I think the pleasure I took derived in part from my never really cutting loose in my teen years.

Part of what made the class great was that it was terra incognita. I had everything to learn from being around the kids. Then they would disappear back into their families and schools and peer groups after an hour – no onerous responsibility involved. Funny thing, though. After they were gone, I sort of missed them.

•

Simply watching them was a joy. I think of Garrett, of the long, loose limbs and the extreme non-eye-contact. Of Jonathan, who got so tired of being cast as Christ in the little dramas the class sometimes was pressured to perform – he had the long hair, the whiskers, the requisite thinness – that he finally got a haircut and shaved. He would slump, speak quietly, but take darting glances at the beautiful girls in the class. I think of John, one of the most gifted kids in a gifted group. One morning when Steve and I were prodding the class to recall the Ten Commandments and John was absent, a girl named Allison said, "This is the kind of time when you want John around." When John did come, his body seemed armored, his face a mask, as if, in speaking, he was reading from a monitor in his head. His mind worked furiously well, though he also sometimes seemed troubled.

The girls dominated. Allison, Jena and Amanda were regulars. Allison was fair, light-skinned, smiley; Amanda was dark, coiled, a rebel in the making. Younger and from another cultural root – Iran – Bita was much, much quieter. At first, Allison's and Jena's seeming toughness cowed me. For weeks, they never even graced me with a glance, much less a full look.

I have described myself as an anthropologist in relationship to them, but here's the truth: I often thought of myself as a baboon sitting at the edge of a human tribe, trying to decode the meaning of gestures, glances, manners and modes – and fighting long odds. There was no way for me to read an American teenager.

Words and ideas were tendered tentatively, cautiously. If Steve and I weren't careful, discussion could dry up in a heartbeat, then run way off-topic. Knowing this, we let off-topic have its way with the class – better that then silence. There was a gentle squirming away by the kids from religious talk, especially God or Jesus talk. One Sunday, Allison started talking about how much science had advanced our understanding of the world. Her implication was that religion couldn't possibly prevail against it – as if the two were somehow at odds. I burst out with something about the magic and mystery and wonder of the scientific view of the world – I may have talked about atoms, I'm not sure – and surprised everybody, even me. (The next week Allison actually quoted me, as if my outburst had somehow registered.) After Sunday school that day, when Steve and I were alone, he confessed, "Sometimes I feel all alone in there." It was almost as if I'd double-crossed him talking about science that way.

I said, "Steve, God's got 'em right where he wants 'em, doubting the whole thing. They can't have faith if they don't earn it. It's not real if it's passed down to them from their parents and they never question it. Real faith comes with struggle. I was out of the church 30 years. Don't worry. All this is supposed to be happening."

But I ached for him. He has this Jimmy Stewart good-guy earnestness and decency. I've seen his picture as a young guy – he's got a big curly Afro – and I know that he, too, went through kicking out the jambs, which is maybe where he got the dash of smartaleckiness he still possesses. It made sense that Steve was worried about the kids' doubts and rejections. It's no wonder that God's first rule is that no other God take precedence over him, because the way you're most likely to jump the ship of faith as a young person is to take up with some other god than God, or some other ideal. Humanism became that for me: It was sensible and defensible and quite chic among the smartest young men in my dormitory. Humanism was a rational pulpit from which to inveigh against racial injustice, for example – an injustice that the Christian religion or most white people's churches, anyway, had abetted.

•

Wedged between childhood and adulthood, morphing from one state to the other, the students couldn't help but be tense, bottled-up, confused. One hour, they wouldn't look at you, while the next they'd be absolutely bare, telling you they got crazy in 6th grade or that God doesn't answer their prayers anymore or that their mother humiliated them last summer.

It is said that four fundamental forces hold the universe together – gravity, electromagnetism and the strong and weak forces that alloy the constituents of atoms. But nobody talks about the Teenage Force, which ruled our Sunday school class. It's the force that makes walls trickle sweat and chairs pulse with hidden life. I get edgy around it, and the edginess feels both good and bad, full of anticipation and desire and thwartedness. In a room with these kids, I time travel back to my own self-conscious adolescence. *I'm childish too!* I want to yell. *So is my buddy Steve here. We still pout! Just ask our loved ones! Hey, we're all walking on eggshells here. We're all playing pretend. We're all the same underneath – insecure, shy, longing for approval. We never outgrow the need to capture hearts, to be heard, to touch and be touched.*

When the kids finally let me into their circle, something melted inside me. A pulse of the paternal? A parenting instinct? (Oh, to be a cool parent!) Or was it simple baboon gratitude at being let a little ways into the tribe? All that, I guess. When Allison finally looked at me for the first time, I could have whooped – though I didn't trust it would ever happen again. I remember the moment: She was reclining on a couch, head propped up on her fist, in one of those lapses of utter unselfconsciousness that kids evince. (She and her sister Emily, in that state of unconsciousness, sometimes curled up together during class, like a mother cat and kitten, and I'd suddenly feel sorry for having denied myself, by my choice not to have kids, this sort of sight.)

Another Sunday, one of the boys confided to me that he didn't think God answered his prayers. He had pulled me aside to confess a burgeoning agnosticism. I got excited and wrote an e-mail asking him if he wanted to talk more about this, but he never wrote back. I didn't know what to think. Was it a baboon error? Was it wrong to assume I could be forthright? Had I scared him with my directness? Should I have waited for him to approach me? I was in a game I didn't have rules for.

•

I was amazed at the way other grownups at Peace Mennonite – parents – would organize and herd the kids. When it was time, around Christmas, for the kids to do a play, there was no discussion of it, no vote – it was a done deal. Naïve about kids, I'm a much easier mark. They could get away with murder, and by conventional lights, they did, eventually.

Near the end of my second year of teaching, Youth Sunday came around. Steve wanted the kids' service to focus on some aspect of Anabaptist history. As soon as he had described his idea to the class, I sensed it was a groaner – something that would require them to muster every smidgen of dutifulness to enact and would bring only the pallid joy of having acted responsibly.

By that time, my role had become pretty clear; to Steve's Jimmy Stewart I played, oh, Steve Allen, maybe. I was informally in charge of rebellion and/or clowning. At a Christmas pageant, for example, that had as one of its themes the love of money, I photocopied U.S. greenbacks at 400 percent, making grotesquely large $20s that might change hands during the play. So I lobbied Steve for something more homemade on Youth Sunday, something that came more directly from the kids' hearts and related more directly to their experience of church. It would be sort of 1960ish: church as a happening.

If they wanted to play the drums, I argued, to signify where they were at, they should go ahead – but try to frame the playing so it meant something to someone outside themselves. If they wanted to lob grenades of doubt at the congregation, they should be able to, I argued. And so when the service shaped up, we had doubts, we had drums, we had readings that were far too long, taken from texts known only to the kids who read them.

The kids brought couches and chairs of every shape and kind from all over the building and arranged them loosely in our church space, adding potted plants here and there, providing an atmosphere that's hard to describe. Their deconstruction of the physical sanctuary was of a piece with the deconstruction of the order of worship, in which such staples as the call to worship, opening hymn, scripture reading and such evaporated. Steve made an opening statement. It was a Pilate-like disavowal of responsibility for the spectacle about to unfold, a statement made with a wan smile that made clear his feelings of disapproval without, I thought, shaming the kids, a good-natured *Whatever*.

Following him, according to the church bulletin, would come electronic music (except Garrett's computer stiffed him); Allison's Theses – one of which was that sermonizing should be replaced by discussion and other forms of interaction between the minister and congregation; drumming and "perhaps a statement," the bulletin said, by Jonathan; selected readings from the *Cryptonomicon*, described on one website as "War and Peace for Nerds," read by John.

"The Faiths of PMC Youth," which came near the end of the service, was the climax. During Sunday school, or by e-mail, I gathered from each kid a statement of where he or she was on the faith journey. I edited these and stripped away the names. Two of the kids, Amanda and Emily, took turns reading the edited statements aloud. Here are snippets:

> *– I guess I have more of a perspective that comes from Wiccan or goddess beliefs. I don't think there's a God up there in the sky. But I do believe that everything is connected – animals and people and all living things – by some kind of force.*
>
> *– Do I believe in God? I would say the ball is currently up in the air. I could go either way. It'd be really great if I could convince myself that God was real.*
>
> *– I don't know that I believe in God, but I believe in fate. I think reincarnation is a possibility. It also depends on the day – sometimes I'm just agnostic.*
>
> *– Sometimes my dad and I will be watching TV. We'll turn to the God channel. There's a guy saying Jesus forgives everyone – and he looks like he needs an exorcist. I don't think God endorses those people.*
>
> *– I'm not a complete atheist because I believe there's a deity of some sort, in some form. Maybe not one who actually exists somewhere "out there" in the universe. It doesn't make sense for somebody to be hanging around up there in space.*
>
> *– I think there's a God and everything. I just really always have believed in God. But I'm not going to be one who's going to church every Sunday. I like hanging out here in Sunday school.*

The statements provoked some angst in Steve. Sometimes I feel a shade guilty about that Sunday. I figure poor Steve thought I had given the inmates the run of the asylum. I believe it was a good thing, though, to give air and light to the doubts that crowd the minds of adolescents as they struggle to keep faith. If we dread the part of us that doubts, we won't have a viable faith. And we need doubters in our midst, too. They force reconsideration and uncomfortable change on those who would turn lively faith into deadly dogma. If we don't permit doubt, the odds go down that keen-minded people will remain in any sort of relationship to God. If there is no room for the kind of skepticism that's instinctive in thinking people, then thinking people will leave the church. Some people need a less orthodox bridge to God – or God on wholly new terms from those of childhood.

A couple of months after the service, Steve and I ended our term as co-teachers. Still feeling a little guilty toward him, I worked on organizing a party in honor of his years of service as a youth Sunday school teacher. I gave him books, wrote a poem and posted his picture, blown up, all over the house where the party was held. He accepted it with warm smiles and his own Jimmy Stewart earnest and quiet goodness.

After the party was over, I walked out to the cul de sac where I'd parked my car, passing Amanda and a couple of others from the class. The day was running out of light. As I passed the group, I felt the usual self-consciousness I feel when I pass a group of teenagers talking about things I sense they want no adult to hear. But Amanda had a surprise for me. She gave me a gift I had not known I was going to get. She said something to me. I don't remember her exact words, but the message was *Roger, you're really cool.*

It's a temptation with a class to pretend that you're the teacher, but the roles of teacher and student can change rapidly, when everything's working. When Amanda said I was cool, I found that I was mistaken about being the resident baboon. I was a member – and maybe even a cool one – of the tribe. Adolescence is a much better experience the second time around.

7.

Welcome

There may be many good reasons to join or remain in a religious community, but a desire for calm consensus, shared values, and a retreat from uncertainty is not among them.

Fred Kniss
Disquiet in the Land

Mennonites are no monolith. Some serve in the military; others are pacifists. Their interpretations of the Bible vary, and they part ways as well over matters like hair and sleeve length, head coverings for women in church, and the display of the American flag. My Mennonite wife, Barbara, says that her great-grandmother belonged to a breakaway Mennonite group called the Wislers. They had an issue with chrome bumpers (deemed too showy), so they painted theirs black.

Nevertheless, the core beliefs of most modern Anabaptists were enunciated in a speech by Harold S. Bender on Dec. 28, 1943, in the chapel of Columbia University. "The Anabaptist Vision" stressed discipleship, which implied to Bender more than experiencing an inner transformation by God's grace. Rather, as with Jews and Quakers, deeds were important to Mennonites, specifically the modeling of one's deeds after Christ's. Bender also spoke of voluntary church membership – not conscription into the faith through infant baptism – and, finally, love and nonresistance.

There's also been stress on the need for congregations to engage in Bible study and to work together to discern, in any given dispute, the correct course of action. One of the loftiest Mennonite ideals is that a congregation should be able to make decisions by consensus.

Achieving consensus requires a group to work patiently toward a unified stand on difficult issues. If that's not possible, those involved in the discussion should, in the opinion of most Mennonites, at least reach a position from which opponents to an idea can comfortably ***stand aside*** from, rather than ***block***, the will of the corporate body without damage to conscience. If consensus is followed strictly, one person can, if resolute enough, block the will of 25 on the other side of an argument (unless, exasperated, the 25 decide to go with a majority rules approach).

The ideal of consensus decision-making is being sorely tested these days. A Faith Communities Today survey, sponsored by the Hartford Institute for Religion Research in 2002, polled 14,300 congregations of many faiths. Seventy-five percent reported some conflict within the preceding five years. Creeping ideology has poisoned many a spiritual family.

Mennonites may be a peace-loving tribe, but they sometimes struggle as much as other brands of churchgoers to get along. It's easier to remember that we must love our distant enemies than to tolerate our irritating neighbors.

Historically, given their commitment to peace, Mennonites tend to flee under stress, dropping out of a church conference, for example, rather than staying and fighting. I, too, am prone to flee when the going gets tough. But I know that if I flee I'm likely – in conversations with allies – to pathologize those who disagree with me. If I can keep my seat, the challenge becomes one of maintaining eye contact with those on the other side of an argument, as well as my ability to reason.

•

Homosexuality has been a hard topic for all churches and denominations to deal with, and Mennonites are no exception. In 1986, '87 and '95, official church statements declared homosexuality a sin but urged church members to remain in "loving dialogue" with homosexuals and their supporters.

In its 1995 statement, the Mennonite Church Council of Faith, Life and Strategy counseled homosexuals to remain celibate and referred to the possibility of "converting" gays to heterosexuality. Then, in 1997, the oldest Mennonite church in the United States, in Germantown, Pennsylvania, was voted out of a southeastern Pennsylvania Mennonite conference. Other Mennonite churches were also expelled or disciplined by conferences before the turn of the millennium, including Kansas City's Rainbow Mennonite Church. Its crime: publishing "welcoming statements" that promised gays and lesbians, bisexuals and transgendered individuals that at Rainbow they'd be treated the same as heterosexuals.

More recently, as acceptance of sexual alternatives has grown, the nature of the battles has changed. In 2010, a San Francisco Mennonite minister was put on probation by Pacific Southwest Conference of Mennonite Church USA. She'd married two men in October 2008. Our minister, Joanna Harader, had to meet with a committee of church officials in Newton, Kansas, in 2010. Committee members wanted to discuss her performance of a "covenant ceremony" for two women earlier that year.

But here I'll tell the story of our church's decision to welcome gays, an action that happened under the leadership of Joanna's predecessor.

•

Whatever side a Christian takes about homosexuality, finding backup in the Bible is a no-brainer. The traditionalist can cite St. Paul's famous attack on homosexuals in Romans 1: 26-27: "Because of this, God gave them over to shameful lusts. Even their women exchanged natural relations for unnatural ones. In the same way the men also abandoned natural relations with women and were inflamed with lust for one another. Men committed indecent acts with other men, and received in themselves the due penalty for their perversion." Paul implies that these "perversions" can be overcome with God's help. In 1 Corinthians 6: 9-11, he warns: "Do not be deceived: Neither the sexually immoral nor idolaters nor adulterers nor male prostitutes nor homosexual offenders nor thieves nor the greedy nor drunkards nor slanderers nor swindlers will inherit the kingdom of God. And that is what some of you were. But you were washed, you were sanctified, you were justified in the name of the Lord Jesus Christ and by the Spirit of our God." In the Old Testament, you can find homosexuals or homosexuality reviled in Leviticus 18 and 20. (Leviticus is also the book in which God attacks those who crossbreed cattle or wear cloth made of two different fibers.)

Church liberals can just as easily find passages to support their positions. Christ's call, for example, to love one's neighbor (as well as God and oneself) and to suspend judgment (judge not, lest ye be judged) seem to point to a need for tolerance. That said, I concede that it's a little disingenuous for Christian liberals (count me among them) to cite chapter and verse in support of their position, for they/we focus more on biblical inconsistency than inerrancy.

So liberals also tend to cite other sources.

Some scientists, for example, are looking for a gay gene or genes as the basis for sexual orientation. Most agree though that besides genetics, a cocktail of influences – including chemistry in the womb and social influences – comes into play. If and when other chemical and biological differences between gays and straights are discovered, it may become easier to say that sexual orientation is biologically driven. If that happens, God's mysterious ways will become even more mysterious.

Whether you embrace or reject LGBT folk depends of course on influences other than science and scripture. It depends on values. A study of 1,236 people who claimed Christianity was central to their identity was reported in the Proceedings of the National Academy of Sciences in 2012. Those who claimed they were "liberals were much more likely to attach greater weight to teaching and tenets involving issues of fellowship," according to the study, "whereas conservatives were somewhat more likely to attach greater weight to teaching and tenets involving issues of morality."

•

Rainbow Mennonite Church, in Kansas City, Kansas, is just an hour's drive away from ours, and the debate about whether to include welcoming language in our bulletin occurred in 2001, engendering fractiousness and pain.

Our relatively few conservative members felt upset and threatened during the debate, experiencing what some homosexuals have experienced: being an unheard minority. On the other side, our liberals were also pained. They viewed themselves as voices crying in a Mennonite wilderness, ashamed of conferences giving the heave-ho to rebel churches like the Germantown church for allowing "sexual minorities into [full] membership," according to that church's website.

During the discussion at Peace, I defended the pained traditionalists – to the disappointment and puzzlement of my liberal friends, who no doubt expected my unwavering support of the principle of equality. But I sometimes care less about principle than about the individual human heart, the same that beats in all of us, the one that's so susceptible to hurt. In this case, I felt that the hearts of the few traditionalists at Peace were hurting more than those on the other side, so I sought to bridge the gap between these partisans.

A sense of the vulnerability of the Others . . . an ability to perceive what we have in common with them . . . little of that seems to happen instinctively. At some point in the distant past, when biological life weighed its needs, it apparently found that rage, fear and judgment served it better than kindness and companionability. But Mennonites have a word for the ability to empathize and overcome the fight/

flight instinct: Gelassenheit, or "yieldedness," meaning surrender of self, submission, humility.

•

In spring 2001, the Peace and Justice Committee invited our church to consider joining the Supportive Congregations Network, which had formed in 1995. SCN was backing outcast Mennonite churches like Rainbow and Germantown. Today, five Kansas Mennonite churches, of a total of 48, are public about welcoming everyone, no matter their sexual orientation or gender identity. So, too, is a Sunday school class at a Mennonite church in north Newton.

SCN requires any group that joins to publicly voice its support for gays. I spoke earlier about the Mennonite ideal of consensus decision-making. It was impossible to achieve that consensus on the decision to join SCN, so the congregants at the meeting voted instead. A majority approved the insertion of this sentence on the weekly bulletin: "As we endeavor to realize the vision of shalom – to embody the wisdom and compassion of Jesus – we welcome into the full life of the church all who similarly aspire, embracing a diversity of race, gender, sexual orientation, economic and life circumstance."

A dispute broke out as our church moved toward this position and these words, and the fight wasn't about the misplaced participial phrase beginning with word "embracing." Was the dispute useful? I would say it was, because it made me wonder how to remain in relationship with those I differed with. All my life, I've avoided conflict because it makes me angry and afraid, sharp-tongued and gossipy. Yet the Gelassenheit ethos demands I turn toward those I disagree with, not away, and do so compassionately.

Sigh.

•

As a professional editor and writer, I pay close attention to public language. So one of my objections to the welcoming statement we finally agreed to was aesthetic. In the laundry list of *protected classes* with which it closes,

I hear the echo of equal opportunity statements and civil suits, which may be perfect for adoption by, say, a university affirmative action board but strike me as legalistic and wooden for a church. (I had, in fact, chaired such a board at the University of Kansas in 1983 when we put similar language into its equal opportunity statement.)

Before the final draft was approved, I had suggested language that seems, in retrospect, windy:

"Welcome to Peace Mennonite Church. Simplicity, service and peace are our abiding values. Hating, excluding, shunning, judging or mocking anyone for any reason is anathema to us. Our sacred text is the Bible. As we wrestle with its contradictions, and with its call to live virtuously, we don't always agree about its meaning. Yet we share a faith that God wants us to live together and to talk peaceably about our differences."

The statement

- defines core Mennonite values (simplicity, service and peace),
- proclaims the need for universal love,
- puts the Bible right out there (a nod to our conservatives),
- acknowledges its contradictions (for our liberals),
- and expresses a willingness to stay in relationship despite disagreements (in the spirit of Gelassenheit).

It gained little support.

•

In opposing the welcoming statement we eventually got, I sided with my fellow youth Sunday school teacher, Steve Unruh. As you learned in the last chapter, Steve's a real Mennonite, with a real Mennonite name and past, and a lifelong devotion to Christianity, except for the usual chaotic spell between ages 18 and 26. He's the kind of guy who's the pulse of the Christian church at its best, the kind who should be at the center, not on the margin. He's got foibles, of course – a certain inattentiveness, at times, that he would acknowledge – but a sharp word has never passed between us and I've never felt judged by Steve, despite our ideological differences.

I tried to support him throughout this controversy because the welcoming statement issue was so painful to him. I'm essentially a liberal; Steve and I both know that. At one point, I stood on my front porch with him and said, "The battle's over, man. By the year 2050 we'll know the genetic markers for homosexuality."

Steve, a Christian psychologist, replied, "I don't know. I think from working with clients that there's often rage at the parents involved in homosexuality." To Steve, homosexuality looks, at times, like a provocative choice – not a destiny. I think childhood experiences could be the basis for some people's homosexuality, but I'm guessing that someday we'll recognize that's a minority.

After the welcoming statement had been approved, I said to Steve, "We have to love these guys on the other side even if we disagree with them, even if we feel marginalized by them." He chuckled, "I've been feeling that way for about 12 years now." He meant in the context of the church. I felt the pain in his smile.

It was cheating to talk that way to Steve – cheating to use the word "we." But I did fight the statement we wound up with, and I did stand with Steve's resistance to it, because, in the end, I thought that the liberal ideals of the statement were too entwined with political spite, with a desire for revenge against the bad guys: the Mennonite conferences. The spirit of the decision-making process felt wrong to me. I sensed that as the discussion unfolded, ideology took too large a bite out of fellow feeling.

•

During the public meeting about joining SCN, a large majority of the 35 to 40 people present favored the idea. A majority was not what we had hoped for, however. Consensus – a 100 percent affirmation – was the goal. A lawyer who'd been coming to our church for a few Sundays at that point told the gathering the day of the meeting that she hoped to see Mennonite consensus-building in action. She left disappointed, because our debate didn't have nearly so satisfying a conclusion. That was the last I saw of her.

The debate began predictably – with the citing of personal experience. One woman said she supported our joining SCN as a way of supporting her lesbian sister and what she had had to endure. Another person, a member of the Peace and Justice Committee, angrily derided someone who had opposed SCN membership. This was, after all, a *political move*, he said. Mennonite churches were being kicked out of Mennonite conferences; joining SCN was a way to protest that. Still another alluded to members of the gay community: "Believe it or not, this vote is a litmus test. Our vote will have consequences. We are being watched."

The rejoinders were equally predictable. Someone said he thought that if we explicitly welcomed lesbians and gays, conservatives would distance themselves from the church. Steve told the group that he thought that SCN had an agenda of erasing St. Paul's equation of homosexuality and sin, and he objected to that.

At this point in the conversation, I was naïve. I thought I struck a mild tone with my question: "Well, couldn't we just say on our church bulletin, 'We welcome everybody'?"

Like, c'mon guys. Can't we just be friends?

A member of the Peace and Justice Committee pounced.

"No!! All kinds of churches say that but they don't really mean it!"

The speaker's words felt like a slap.

"But we DO mean it," I sputtered. "Just because somebody uses those words and doesn't mean them, doesn't affect the words. We can REALLY mean them, can't we?"

I thought about George Orwell's *1984*, about the distortions of language under the mythical Big Brother – war is peace, freedom is slavery. I thought, *Since when does "We welcome everyone" mean "We stick to our own kind, thanks"? Our church isn't like that!* I felt my neck getting hot.

"I don't think there's **anyone** sitting here who would turn a gay man or a lesbian away from our church," I continued, "or be less than welcoming. There's a deeper issue here, and it has to do with our sacred text. Let's face it: Not every gay or lesbian is going to feel comfortable with the Bible, given what St. Paul says.

"There's the physical church – the building – and then there's the invisible church, the REAL church, the one that's got a history, understandings, rules. It fractures over every little thing.

"We can say whatever words we want to on our bulletin, welcome gays and lesbians into our physical church, but that won't change the Bible or the tradition or the contention between political factions in the church, which is where the deeper issue lies, I think. That's why I'm in favor of a more general welcome to all."

Someone on the Peace and Justice Committee said, "Well, the SCN requires that we *explicitly* welcome gays and lesbians. We can't join SCN with just a general welcoming statement."

I said, "Then I oppose joining SCN, because I don't think we should give away our right to use the words we wish to use to express our convictions. To express the complex truth of who we are."

The lawyer who came to see Mennonite consensus-building in action was sitting on my left. She said to the group, "If you're upset with conferences for dictating terms of membership and throwing churches out, why would you join a new organization that wants to dictate language to you?"

And so it went. After a couple of hours those in charge of the meeting gave up on consensus and the issue of whether to join SCN came to a vote. Fifteen people cast a ballot in favor of joining SCN. Six, including the pastor, "stood aside." Two other members, one of them Steve, cast votes against the measure. About half of those present, myself included, couldn't vote. We weren't, at that point, members of the church.

Some of those who'd urged the congregation to join SCN seemed dismayed, despite their victory. One woman rose to say, with great passion, that if it weren't for 250 years worth of women who had struggled for women's rights, she might not be rising to speak at all. And then she wept as she told the circle she was bitterly disappointed we had not reached consensus.

•

The guy who welcomed me enthusiastically the day I first came to Peace called me an "enigma" after that meeting. I only wish he'd asked me to clarify my enigmatic position. Another person at the meeting said, in an implicit reference to me, that he was no "card-carrying intellectual." Maybe my way of approaching the problem was too heady. As a reporter who then attended Peace and since has moved said, "There's not a lot of room for nuance in this discussion."

It's true: I am an intellectual and perhaps, occasionally, enigmatic. I've always been a bit of a contrarian. But I also think a church should provide a haven for every outcast, downtrodden and scorned minority and ethnic group. A church is a great place to practice 360-degree tolerance and understanding.

I had watched Steve teach teenagers every Sunday for a couple of years. What radiates from him are delight and love, as well as a longing for them to cleave to the faith. He reads his own faults clearly; when he is petty, he catches the whiff of it; when he is angry, he doesn't nurse it. There's no hate in the guy.

And he's humble. When, during the SCN meeting, Steve saw he was on the losing side of this issue, he asked the congregation in a friendly tone to consider whether they wanted him to teach Sunday school. Everybody laughed. Steve's virtues are well-established. But he wasn't kidding.

•

Someone who had been coming to Peace for years helped me make historical sense of what happened. The church's first pastor, a man named John Linscheid, had come out at Peace Mennonite in 1983. The congregation was divided about this but retained him as an interim pastor. The Western District Conference, to which Peace belongs, demanded he be ousted if the church wanted to receive continued financial support. Here is what the long-time member wrote to me.

I see this discussion as a continuation of discussions over the years about the direction of PMC. The church was started by several families with different views about Christianity within the Mennonite framework. The church lost a bunch of the more conservative members when the first pastor came out. The second pastor hired was a woman. Since then the church has stabilized, but with an uneasy sense of identity. When we interviewed pastors before we hired Rod [Stafford, a Peace pastor in the 1990s], our first choice decided not to come here because we did not have a clear identity. He saw trouble. Smart man.

Rod was a good fit, I think – personally conservative but he worked hard to make the more liberal folks feel welcome and included. But we still had different 'camps' of folks, and there was another split of sorts between those who had kids and those who didn't.

This welcoming statement is all the more difficult because of this unclear identity, I think. So I believe the dialog has been a valuable process. It has helped define who we are.

Maybe our church will be a place where conservative Mennonites are not comfortable – welcome, yes, but not comfortable. I don't know if that's good or bad. I don't know how you can create a place that's comfortable for both conservatives and homosexuals. I'd sure love to see it happen if it could.

•

The welcoming statement was finished in a couple of months, drafted by three members of the Peace and Justice Committee. Before its approval, Steve made one final effort to modify its language by writing to the church listserv. He referred to the fact that no one who voted against joining SCN had been invited to participate in drafting the welcoming-statement language.

"I know that in the past, the church has not generally entertained 'write-in' drafts in church policy-making," Steve wrote. "However, given that, to my knowledge, dissenters in the recent vote to establish a significant position that our church will be taking were not invited to participate in authoring this potentially divisive position, perhaps the church should, in fairness, consider an option."

Steve asked, in his e-mail, whether we might, in the welcoming statement, acknowledge that we "sin and fall short of the Glory of God" as individuals but nevertheless "press on to the mark" and "run the good race."

He also suggested these words: "As a congregation, we welcome into the full life of the church you who believe your hope and salvation rests in Jesus Christ, and we welcome you regardless of life circumstance, including sexual orientation."

Steve ended by saying that he opposed the statement that had been proposed (which is pretty much what we wound up adopting in the end). He apologized for being unable to attend the upcoming meeting where a vote on it would occur – he was taking a quick trip to Colorado with his wife's mother.

While the "hope and salvation rests in Jesus Christ" part gave me a touch of queasiness, I was encouraged that Steve's statement explicitly referred to sexual orientation, which was one of the SCN requirements. I could see he was giving ground. So I wrote the following to the listserv:

"To All Who Attend Peace Mennonite:

"I think Steve Unruh's suggestion is a good compromise. He's fused language that reflects a traditional commitment of Christians everywhere to Christianity's namesake with language that acknowledges our 21st century understanding of sexual orientation. . . ."

One church member didn't like my seconding Steve's position. He phoned to chew me out:

"I frankly think you're being disingenuous. I can't see how you could possibly agree with Steve. In my opinion, you're trying to prong the congregation."

My morale was low by then, and the charge bit. I was stuck in a confusing place. One part of me felt protective toward Steve, while another part felt that singling out gays for sexual doctoring was a grossly loveless position for a Christian to take. I choked up as we talked, defending my integrity, asserting that I did, indeed, believe that the infusion of the spirit of Christ into my heart had been slow and painful and utterly necessary to achieving whatever measure of goodness I had achieved. Making Christ a head trip – emphasizing his role as wisdom teacher – was, for some of us (like Steve), too little, I said. Our identification with Jesus had to be more radical, had to reach deeper into the central nervous system and produce a more profound alteration.

Toward the end of the conversation, the other fellow apologized. There was a wound, and it took time to heal. But later I warmed to him again. On the other hand, the person who called me an "enigma," whom I initially felt closer to when I came to the church – we never regained our former footing.

Both have since left the church. Steve and I stayed.

•

After the vote to join SCN, I wrote a member of the Peace and Justice Committee. I told her I was thinking of writing a magazine article about our church's decision. I said, "I'd like to know your thoughts and deliberations in moving toward the decision you made to cast a 'yes' vote" to join the SCN.

She wrote back, "I can understand your interest in wanting to write an article about our church process, but I wonder if it doesn't make sense, at this point, for the coordinating committee or related committee to contact the local and Mennonite press."

To me, that didn't make sense. That approach seemed more in the style of a hierarchical church than ours. One of the appeals of the Mennonite church is its flattened hierarchy. I kept silent, deciding to wait. The next day she wrote to the minister and me: "I'm concerned about an article being written for publication about the process before the process has been completed. . . . I'm happy to speak to the world openly about this issue and I'm even interested in sharing my ideas and concerns about the process – it just feels too soon."

A few months later, just before the congregational meeting that authorized the final welcoming statement, I tried again. I ran into her at the local food co-op, and she said that some of those who'd drafted the language had thought about meeting personally with Steve and me.

When would I be free? she asked.

I was happy to be asked. Touching base in a live conversation would help. I told her I'd be available that evening and the next day, too. I'd be glad to take time off from work, if that fit into others' schedules, to talk about the statement.

The next day I got this e-mail:

"When I saw you yesterday I mentioned the possibility of a meeting with you and Steve and the statement committee. Where that's at now is that [one of those who drafted the statement] was going to call Steve and we'll have that meeting only if Steve feels like he needs to meet with us. If you have additional comments or questions or concerns, do feel free to call me or [the other member of the statement committee]. Otherwise bring your ideas to the congregational meeting on Sunday and we can all look at them at that time. Thanks – take care."

Was there fear of an emotional exchange in a personal setting? I don't know, but something started to freeze in me. I decided not to go to the Sunday meeting. I chose to flee rather than fight.

•

After the welcoming statement was finalized, I wrote to those who drafted the statement.

I'm writing about the SCN welcoming-statement process for a book I've been working on.

As part of this, because you were on the committee that put the statement together, I'd like you to write about your thinking in regard to the final statement.

1. Who are the target audiences of the welcoming statement in its final form? What is the subtext of the welcoming statement for those audiences?

2. Beyond welcoming people of various genders, race, economic circumstance and sexual orientation to the church, what do you believe that we, as a church, should do, if anything, to actively bring people of color, poor people and gays and lesbians through the doors of Peace Mennonite Church? What do you see yourself doing, personally, to help our church become more diverse? Is it more important, in your opinion, to extend a welcome or to actively seek diversity?

3. If a fundamentalist Christian were to walk through the doors of our church next Sunday morning and rise, during sharing, to quote St. Paul and the Book of Romans to us on the subject of homosexuality, and then condemn us, would you approach him to welcome him to our church? If not, why not? If you did, what would you say to him?

I look forward to hearing from you.

The third question was a jab I couldn't resist, and that may help explain why I didn't get a straight answer from anyone. "I'm happy to talk with you about all those questions," wrote one, "but not interested in being part of a book." Another responded: "Roger, I'm sorry I've not gotten back with you till now. I've been pretty tied up with [other things] for the last two weeks. As I get free of that, I intend to give your e-mail some more thought. I'll give you a call when I've had a chance to do that." I never got that call, though the caller did approach me in church one day, and we had a nice chat. I continue to like him, even if

I am an enigma to him; I suspect he likes me, too. A third person didn't reply.

•

Multiply our church's pain by that in all the churches deliberating about this issue, and that's a whole lot of hurt.

In the book *What's So Amazing about Grace?* Philip Yancey writes, "The church has allowed itself to get so swept up in political issues that it plays by the rules of power, which are rules of ungrace. In no other arena is the church at greater risk of losing its calling than in the public square." Yancy was talking about right wing evangelicals, but fundamentalism of any political stripe – and politics in general – tends to be dis-graced, un-graced or whatever you want to call it. Politics leads to tribalism and division.

Divisions are inevitable. The key is hanging tough when that happens, not picking up your marbles and going home – and not killing the poor minister forced to weather tidal waves of disagreement, either. At first, I resisted running away. But about a year after the vote I found myself feeling hurt, and I took a "sabbatical" of a few months. I felt humbled, and I didn't like it a bit, and it seemed important to stay away and sulk.

Despite all that, I have an ideal of a church in my mind's eye – a place where everybody keeps showing up, ready and willing to struggle through difficult and conflicting feelings. In my ideal church, for every person who thinks homosexuality is a sin and an abomination in the eyes of the Lord, there'd be another pointing out that Christ would have us love all humans even-handedly. For every person who thinks that African Americans are the accursed offspring of Ham, another would be spiritedly color-blind. We would have to lower our voices as we talked. Or perhaps, until such an exchange became tolerable, we might just sit quietly together, living with our disagreements and still respecting each other.

Why? Because such behavior has the potential for enlarging the spirit.

I didn't come back to church after 32 years away in order to network. I came back knowing how much unfinished business I still had to do. One piece of that is a deep reluctance to give up the pleasure of disdain.

Around Here Somewhere

George Muller's is a case extreme in every respect, and in no respect more so than in the extraordinary narrowness of the man's intellectual horizon. His God was, as he often said, his business partner. . . . When we compare a mind like his with such a mind as, for example, Emerson's or Phillips Brooks's, we see the range which the religious consciousness covers.

William James
Varieties of Religious Experience

We find so much diversity in how people describe what is religious and spiritual to them.

Andrew Newberg
Principles of Neurotheology
National Public Radio/December 15, 2010

8.

A Peekaboo God?

The third step of recovery in the 12-step path of Alcoholics Anonymous reads, "Made a decision to turn our will and our lives over to the care of God as we understood him." An AA member once told me, "God might be a tree you have a special relationship to." The words "as we understood him" (or her or it) signify how important it was to the founders of AA that individuals be allowed to find terms in which to make God meaningful.

God has been understood in so many ways that confusion is appropriate. The descriptors of the God are plentiful: omniscient, omnipresent, omnipotent, transcendent, imminent; love, the way, the truth, the light and the bringer of light; the word and the word made flesh; Father, Son and Holy Spirit. God is the harsh master of Ezekiel, forcing the prophet to eat a scroll on which are inscribed woes and lamentations to be visited upon the rebellious Israelites; God is a tender-hearted being who loved humans enough to have incarnated into someone who inspired awe, betrayal and slaughter; God has a plan for our lives . . . or is the engineer of the universe who, after its creation, withdrew . . . or is utterly unknowable.

Forget the mysterious trinity for a moment. As the son, God is richly varied: both human and divine; a precocious boy with a mind that lets him run rings around his elders;

a tenderhearted man who counsels that we must love, love, love – even those who persecute us; a hothead who turns over the tables of money changers; a strict leader who tells those who would follow to prepare to leave their families and personal histories behind; and, in the end, a being sufficiently humble to yield to his destiny – though not without a tiny bit of whining.

So far I've sampled but a smattering of the theological conceptions of God. But God is yeasty enough that even the secular glom onto him. The spiritually inclined who pooh-pooh a personal God often experience the "divine" in nature. Those who live more in their intellect (physicists, for example) may sense God's handiwork in the extraordinarily narrow set of conditions under which our universe formed: conditions within which, on our small planet, life could hatch from a stew of inorganic material, crawl onto land and ultimately evolve into many different kinds of beings, including one in Kansas typing these words and another one somewhere else reading them. That a primate descended from simple sea creatures would be thinking about this seems, to some Christians, vanishingly small.

The indirect "evidence" for God, if it can be called that, is larger, to my way of thinking, than any direct sign. To a mind ready to believe, God is there in the sudden surprise or coincidence and in the especially meaningful dream; in the still, small voice inside that nudges us toward or away from something; or in the numinous remark made at the lesbians-only Codependents Anonymous meeting or by the stranger at the grocery store.

The fact that God is near to some, far away to others, and can come from a multiplicity of directions increases the sense of mystery. Is God as near as an artery . . . or as distant as the edge of a universe created by an explosion of what was in theory a point of super-dense matter many, many times smaller than the question mark at the end of this sentence? Is God a mechanic who started the universe ticking and then split, as the Enlightenment had it, or an ongoing meddler? Or something in between? Or something else entirely?

Try this one on: It is thought by physicists that the long theorized and recently discovered Higgs boson forms a medium within which all matter rests. They believe the Higgs field is the source of that quality of matter we call "mass." Is God, like the Higgs field, a medium – one that lends the events of life a quality called "meaning"?

•

Personally, I find the question of whether God interacts with us frequently, occasionally, rarely or not at all among the most fascinating. A 2005 survey by Baylor University scholars showed that the answer depends to some extent on gender and education: Women and people with less education on average tended to envision a more engaged God than men and people with more education, for example.

Many fundamentalist Christians think God is closely woven into our lives. In fact the idea of God as a being who breathes down our necks (or keeps a census of our hairs) is pervasive, such that even secular-minded folks will often tell you that "everything happens for a reason." I instinctively mistrust that claim. It seems to me to cheapen our human efforts. God as puppeteer is the worst of all the available models, I think.

My mother once shared a log with me. It was given to her by a friend at church and was written by the friend's daughter. The daughter lives far from the mother and attends a different church. The daughter thinks God is very, very near. To both my mother and her friend, the log seemed odd.

The woman's husband hears his name spoken in the night, sees bright lights, wakes up to deep, inner trembling, hears the Lord whisper numbers to him. He takes these numbers as reading assignments, tasking him to look at certain pages in his Bible.

In the log, the woman writes: "The Glory Cloud filled our home. I mean a real cloud. Not an imaginary cloud . . . the real, tangible cloud of Glory that you can see, feel, and even touch. This has happened to [us] several times before . . . and we have experienced it together, at the same time.

In the kitchen where we were talking, in the living room, upstairs, it was everywhere!!!"

Reports like this fill me with unkind thoughts. I want to say, Don't you dare imagine God as a ghost floating around your house! I'm far more sympathetic to Thomas Aquinas' labors of logic over the more than two hundred volumes of the *Summa Theologica*, work that was interrupted by a mystical experience shortly before his death. In 1293 he said to someone who urged him to continue to write: "I can do no more. Such secrets have been revealed to me that all I have written now appears to be of little value." I'm one of those who thinks that glory clouds, if they appear at all, as they finally did for Aquinas, should be earned with the sweat and strain of years passed on the rock pile of doubt. I realize that this thought is wrong-headed, that giving more weight to grace also gives more credit to God. Obviously, I'm the kind of person who roots for the older brother in the story of the Prodigal Son. Good Brother, hoping that virtuous labor and duty will be rewarded, stays home to help Dad with the family farm while Prodigal Son's out squandering his inheritance. Good Brother seethes when Prodigal gets a huge welcome home by Dad – and I seethe with him.

Aquinas had a great mind, but he couldn't find a close-up God with it for many years, which leads to this question: Why is the human mind such a poor searchlight for God? I imagine the mind's ability to see paradoxes and to second-guess itself explains a lot of that. And yet, ironically, second-guessing the self is the basis for conscience, so the ability serves God in at least one way.

When it comes to actually experiencing God, however, there can be no second-guessing. Faith, like going to the theatre, requires that we suspend disbelief, that we let go of doubt, at least for a while. Yet in that relinquishment, our moral awareness may begin to fog over. We have seen in our time how extremes of faith and lack of self-doubt can produce, at minimum, mischief.

On the other hand, bringing too much mind to the search for God, we risk reducing God to lowercase letters and draining God of mystery. Erich Fromm in *The Art of Loving* notes that through the millennia, man has abstracted God more and more. The far reach of such abstraction is to conclude that God IS truth and God IS love. This is close to saying that Love IS God and Truth IS God, at which point the divine is eclipsed by the merely virtuous.

My response is to continue to imagine that God is unimaginable, ungraspable and irreducible. I put God on a mountain several time higher than Everest, on a pinnacle where the sun never shines. My mind cannot see there, yet I turn my gaze in the direction of that dark mountain again and again.

•

I say that "I put God on a mountain" but seeing God in this way isn't wholly a matter of will or of reason.

Cool Hand Luke, in the 1960s movie of the same name, escapes from prison, is hunted by his jailers, then cornered by them in a church. They're outside and he's in. He looks toward the ceiling and tries talking to God. For the whole flick, Luke's been dogged by the authorities for petty infractions; now he wants the Real Authority to say something. No answer comes, so Luke sticks his head out the church window and shouts to the prison warden, "What we have here is a failure to communicate!"

The warden has used the same line on Luke before subjecting him to various cruel punishments, so this is a taunt – aimed at both warden and God. Luke is shot dead without ever having heard what Martin Marty would call "the Yes of an awakening, responsive God."

Marty, in *A Cry of Absence: Reflections for the Winter of the Heart*, writes that God's silences must sometimes simply be borne: "The sense of spiritual abandonment comes with such frequency [in the Book of Psalms] that all who believe in God must be ready to experience it." Yet Marty makes a virtue of God's not gratifying us with a clear response to prayer, arguing that it heightens our sensitivity to a response. "Precisely in the context of those Psalms where passions are most intense, the depth most threatening, the winters longest and most cold – there it is that the Yes of an awakening, responsive God is noticed."

C.S. Lewis, in *A Grief Observed*, says that God's "silence" may not be silence at all but a phantom. Perhaps when we suffer, the noise of our turmoil drowns God out: "The time when there is nothing at all in your soul except a cry for help may be just the time when God can't give it: You are like the drowning man who can't be helped because he clutches and grabs. Perhaps your own reiterated cries deafen you to the voice you hoped to hear."

That sounds like blaming the victim to me, but then God's silence is more disturbing to some of us than to others. We all have our own Room 101, right? That's where, in the book *1984*, the forces of state authority take you to break you by confronting you with your worst fear. My Room 101 is having a relationship in which there is an ongoing emotional entanglement with someone I'm no longer on speaking terms with, a relationship in which warmth and light have been replaced by dead air. I'm speaking of an unsettling, fraught silence that is stitched with fear, anger, guilt and hurt. I've been vulnerable to this kind of silence ever since childhood, when my father would get mired in depression that I (wrongly) took personally. Sometimes, his silent withdrawals from the family roared like whitewater. This is why, today, when people I love withdraw in silence, without explanation, or when I withdraw from them (into a silence meant to be punishing and hurtful), there's a grim edge to it.

I've found it hard to take responsibility for being a collaborator in forging pained silences. Yet if scientists are right, the limbic area of the brain contains templates for the brands of human connection we habitually tend to seek out. What creates those templates? Childhood experiences of mother, father and siblings, among others. Thus, love may as easily come to mean "being without" as "being with" – or some uneasy mix of the two.

The face of love my father showed included alternating currents of manic warmth, silence and unpredictable rage.

So as an adult I associate being "in love" with wide emotional swings. When it comes to "falling in love," it may be that we possess radar for those who can be coaxed to dance with us in a familiar way. If we fed on struggle sandwiches in life's first years, then the chemistry of love will require, to some extent, struggle – at least until we discover the pattern of our self-undermining behavior.

In short, we may unknowingly seek or create silences that hurt – between us and our love, between us and God.

•

In light of the unnerving quiet some of us experience with a "personal" God, one response is to put a scientific face on the divine. God can be transformed into the head engineer of creation; author of nature's laws; orchestrator of the Big Bang; engineer, brakeman and switchman of evolution; author of the genetic code. For centuries, science has been edging onto God's turf, and God hasn't seemed to mind. God seems (to me) to be more and more modest in his demands for space and attention.

The discoveries of science have been remarkable. They have led some spiritually inclined people to experience feelings of religious awe after exposure to scientific findings, usually mediated by popularizers who may appear glib to scientists. Among the most alluring scientific speculations to the theologically minded are the fantastic cosmological coincidences that make life possible. If certain initial conditions at the time of the Big Bang had been only slightly different, physicists say, then stars, molecules and people would not exist. The "anthropic principle" is a coinage that describes the exceedingly tight specs the universe had to meet for human life as we know it to emerge. If you tinker even slightly with the numbers associated with the four fundamental forces of nature – electromagnetism, gravity and the strong and weak nuclear forces (which account for the stability of atoms) – there'd be 300,000,000,000,000,000,000,000 stars out of business, not to mention the Higgs field and humanity. The same holds if the Big Bang had been only a bit louder and rifled matter out in every direction just a bit faster.

A universe with more than four dimensions would also have caused problems. Cosmologist Stephen Hawking has noted that the effect on the planets' orbits around stars and electrons' orbits around the nucleus would be unstable: "Thus, intelligent life, at least as we know it, could exist only in four dimensions."

In sum, within the "strong anthropic principle" (there is a weak version as well), with its emphasis on the just-so conditions necessary for the emergence of life on Earth, there's a ghost of intelligent design flitting about, a sense that everything happens for a reason (here we go again) on a cosmic scale – and that reason is us. Dale Kohler, a fictional creation of John Updike in the book *Roger's Version,* is a proponent of the strong anthropic principle. Yet what happens to Kohler suggests that Updike is skeptical about plundering scientific discoveries for evidence of God.

Kohler, an earnest student, tries to galvanize Roger Lambert, a theology professor whose spirituality has become a husk:

"Dr. Lambert, aren't you excited by what I've been trying to describe? God is breaking through. They've been scraping away at physical reality all these centuries, and now the layer of the little left we don't understand is so fine God's face is staring right out at us. . . . If God in fact created the universe, then as a fact it has to show, eventually. Let me put it another way: God can't hide any more."

Lambert opposes the idea of God's peeking out: "If God wanted His tracks discovered, wouldn't He have made them plainer?"

Updike, in a *New Yorker* essay published 13 years after *Roger's Version*, said that "the 'anthropic principle,' in its strongest form, holds . . . that the universe was designed to create us; it does not say why an omnipotent God would choose to breed an intelligent species by such a lengthy, wasteful, and cruel method as evolution. Theistic exercises in science and logic . . . may fortify the already persuaded but will not convert disbelievers. . . . No religion is apt to be founded on cold reason. It takes faith out of the equation. Belief, like love, must be voluntary."

Indeed, though it is tempting to try to use science to track down and characterize God, the God that's found by such means isn't emotionally satisfying. If the glory cloud is too close for comfort, the God who thought to calibrate the universe so precisely that it was bound to cough up humanity seems too far away.

•

Maybe I have fervor envy when it comes to fundamentalists. The fundamentalist God inhabits low hills upon which the sun perpetually shines. The trails to Him are well marked: do this, don't do that. So are the bogs – with skulls-and-crossbones.

Yet if I were visited by a glory cloud, I think it would be bad news. I'm already awfully opinionated and pushy about some things. I tell people what books on relationship maintenance they need for their ailing marriages. How it's nuts that the citizens of the United States have trillions in credit card debt but love "reality" TV. How the fact that the majority of the members of the Congress are millionaires means that they're not like the 99 percent of the U.S. public who aren't, and they need, therefore, to be evicted from office. We don't really want folks as sure of themselves as me to have strong religious convictions, do we? Don't we have enough of them already?

So I'm stuck with a high-altitude God, one who lives on a pinnacle that's all dark and foggy, in a set like you might find in an old black-and-white Ingmar Bergman film. A God in some ways like my depressed dad hunkered down in the dark on the living room couch.

One approach, I think, to the problem of defining and locating a distant-if-not-absent God is to take the C.S. Lewis and Martin Marty approach to rationalizing God's silence, which I described earlier. Thomas Merton says in *Contemplative Prayer*: "The true contemplative . . . remains empty because he knows that he can never expect or anticipate the word that will transform his darkness into light. . . . He waits on the Word of God in silence, and when he is 'answered,' it is not so much by a word that bursts into his silence. It is by his silence itself suddenly, inexplicably revealing itself to him as . . . full of the voice of God."

If I REALLY stretch, I can imagine this silence as an expression of love – of a divine patience that is waiting for us humans to get it. In *Roger's Version*, theologian Lambert tells Kohler, "A God Who is a mere fact will just sit there on the table with all the other facts; we can take Him or leave Him. The way it is, we are always in motion toward the God who flees, the *Deus absconditus*; He by His apparent absence is always with us."

Of all the ideas about God, that of the *Deus absconditus* conforms most closely to my experience. This God keeps me in the hunt but frustrates my wish for certainty. By this game of hide-and-seek, I imagine myself being coaxed toward surrender and trust, knowing that if I learn about these qualities, I will then find the still, wonderful heart of faith.

If you're one of those to whom God does not even mumble, much less scold, lecture or nurture, imagining that you're dealing with *Deus absconditus* may be one way to diminish the sting. The notion of such a God was fashionable in the Middle Ages, according to Karen Armstrong, writing in *A Case for God*. Apophatic theology, she says, emphasizes God's unknowability. Aquinas and Meister Eckhart were of this mind. The theology of our age is cataphatic; it has no trouble listing the characteristics of God.

Assigning attributes to the divine makes sense; we seek to explain the inexplicable. But certain attributions are hard to live up to, even for gods. Others are horribly reductive. For someone who wants a showy or splashy God, the idea of a peekaboo god may seem an absurdity or worse – a cruel joke, a theological taunt. Disappointed, some strike out in new directions, turning over stones until they find alternate sources of awe.

But me, I'm taking my hint from Armstrong.

Even if it's not satisfying.

9.

God's Choke Chain

In middle age, some of us imagine duck-nibbling symptoms of possible ill health to be the beginning of cataclysms. Today's fear is blindness, so I'm typing with my eyes shut. Best to ration my sight.

What triggered this fear? My eyes feel parched. They're swollen. They ache. There's a pressure at the bridge of the nose, another at the temples. I need no evidence to imagine a dark future: white cane and a docile dog transforming me into a supermarket spectacle, people with thought bubbles over their heads – *Poor man!* – as I pass.

And I wonder, *Is it all the hours spent at the word processor? Is the fluid inside my eyes turning into jello? Is it deeper – a want of one or another neurotransmitter, a blinking out of nerve cells dedicated to the eye? That sensation back of my ear just then – what was THAT?* I share this anxiety with a friend. He politely asks whether I've also experienced the back problems associated with sustained sitting before a computer.

I think, *I'm going blind, and you ask after my back?*

But I'm crafty enough to respond casually and then guide him back to my fears. "People who stare at computer terminals blink less," I say, adding that my optometrist has instructed me to blink more as I sit at the terminal.

Seems a bit like trying to remember to digest, I think. *I'd rather the autonomic nervous system handle these affairs.*

"Hmmmm," my friend says.

My physician is equally unmoved.

"You know, Roger," he says, "sometimes when things are bothering us, we focus on them and then they seem worse than they really are." He mentions his own foible of having trouble with his eyes for weeks after getting new glasses.

He gives me an all-clear and then suggests an ophthalmologist, whom I'll be able to ask about macular degeneration and other diseases I've been reading about on the web. (There's one whose Swedish-sounding name I can't recall just now.) Maybe, just maybe, something unbearably nasty has skulked into my immune system, as happened to a friend whose body began to reject an eye. Maybe I've come down with blepharospasm; its victims find it impossible to open their eyelids. Is that the arc I'm following?

•

The panic I've just described happened about two decades ago.

My darkest fantasy involved a brain tumor, perhaps because around that time, the forebrain of a professor I'd had in graduate school – a lively, handsome D.H. Lawrence scholar who'd just had a true crime book published – unraveled. He didn't live long after that.

Now I didn't know that brain tumors were linked to the symptoms I've described – no need to allay fear with fact. The imagining of tumors may have been natural given that my father died of cancer, and for years I had lived a life that was, in some ways, a carbon copy of his. We both had fierce energy, and a capacity for laser focus. We shared the same brand of hostility, and I always figured it might do me in, as (I imagined) it had him.

I was in midlife when I began to suspect that my drivenness might be my ruin. My first thought, remembering how cancer's incubation, from the first jumping gene to the last gasp, takes decades, was *Oh, no, it's too late. The damage has been done.*

None of this stopped me from stressing or raging. Nor did therapy, contemplative prayer, mindfulness meditation, anti-depressants or exercise. In the movie *Waterdance*, actor Wesley Snipes colors his new life in a wheelchair in the rosiest hues, but as the movie wears on, he drifts into sullenness. He thought he had exorcised rage; in fact, its residue starts to kill him. Just so, I feared that the incomplete work of expunging anger would catch up with me, that my dry eyes foreshadowed something far worse.

Beyond the dread of my genetic endowment, there was a moral coloring to my anxiety. During a couple of years in the early 1980s a boss had made me miserable, and I tried to return the favor. Eventually, she fired me. A few years later, she died of a brain tumor. Because each of us had tormented the other, I imagined suffering the same fate. Maybe I even *deserve* it, I thought, given all my malicious gossip against her.

Cosmic Scorekeeper is one of God's faces. I'm talking about the God who throws lightning bolts at the wicked, the God children are warned about. If you leave religion behind before a more nuanced idea of God has time to grow, you may be stuck with the cosmic-scorekeeper God. During the years I was out of church and faith, I secretly dreaded God's using disease and disability like you use a choke chain on a dog – to pull me up short, to cinch me to him. I might not find God credible, but still imagined He'd punish me, not only for malice toward my boss but for failing to love my fellow man in sufficient degree . . . for failing to make the full leap of faith to Him . . . for ignoring some of the Ten Rules. I may have been a full-grown 20th century man with a master's degree, but Jonathan Edwards' sermon *Sinners in the Hands of an Angry God*, delivered in 1741, resonated emotionally:

"The bow of God's wrath is bent, and the arrow made ready on the string, and justice bends the arrow at your heart, and strains the bow, and it is nothing but the mere pleasure of God, and that of an angry God, without any promise or obligation at all, that keeps the arrow one moment from being made drunk with your blood."

Fortunately, competing ideas about God have taken hold in me since then.

•

The day of my appointment with the ophthalmologist arrived.

She shined blue lights and white ones into my eyes. She had me look at the ceiling and the floor, rolled back my eyelids and stared at their undersides.

She dropped liquid anesthetics on the eyeballs, then attached two narrow strips of absorbent paper, about the length and breadth of book matches, to the lower lid of each. She left the room. When a timer went off, she came back to the room and removed the strips. Eyes that produce tears in the right volume should wet the strips to a distance of 10 millimeters in five minutes. In my case, an area no bigger than a match head had been dampened.

I wasn't producing enough tears.

"Dry eyes," she said.

"I know," I said, "but what's wrong?"

"It's a condition called dry eyes," she said. "That's all."

But why?

Normal aging of glands in the eye, she answered.

"Better than a brain tumor," I joked.

She looked puzzled, then smiled, as if she knew it was an inside joke.

•

At the time, I sighed relief that God wasn't ready to take me down, and pretty soon after that I stopped thinking about God. Of course other challenges followed. I took a test for early-onset Alzheimer's after suffering the memory loss typical of those in their early 50s. Later, I learned a lot about essential tremor, Parkinson's and other sources of palsy when I developed a mild shake. I repeatedly failed to get out Occam's razor and default to the simplest explanation for these health worries: aging.

Today, I just can't see God as the Cosmic Scorekeeper or Keeper of the Sinner Census. These identities lack subtlety, mystery or interest – qualities I have begun to suspect God has in spades. Sometimes one of our cats, Mattie, gives Barbara a gentle tap on the nose in the morning with its paw. It's her way of saying, "Open the can, Mom." I think Mattie's a better metaphor for God than Jonathan Edwards' Bowman and His blood-drunk arrows.

If God taps us on the nose, it may be startling but it's not dangerous. God may only be telling those who have such experiences that she's hungry for their company.

10.

Is God Flow?

If you're reading these words, you're unlikely to be the kind of person who has to worry about dengue fever or clan warfare. You're probably as warm or cool as you want to be, own a TV of the style and dimensions of your choice. Your belly is full or will be soon.

Those are just guesses, but here's a fact:

If you're an older working American, your average per capita income has more than doubled since 1964, even taking inflation into account.

And here's a question:

Why aren't you happier? Statistics show that in the past half-century, despite becoming more moneyed than ever, we've never had more than 30 to 35 percent of the population calling itself "very happy."

More puzzlers:

- If you win a million dollars in the lottery, within a year to 16 months, you'll be no happier than you were before you got rich.
- If you become a paraplegic, your happiness sinks for a year – and then returns to its previous level.

Why does circumstance do so little to move us toward permanent happiness or sadness? A scholar named Mihali

Csikszentmihalyi has been thinking about this for decades. He's studied visual artists, musicians, chess players, writers – people who happily keep doing their thing even if they don't make much money. He has concluded that their happiness lies in what he calls the "flow experience."

The experience is available to all of us. Remember, as a kid, being transfixed in the sandbox or on the hopscotch grid? Then you've had a taste of flow. When you're in flow, says Csikszentmihalyi, here's what you experience.

- You are totally and ecstatically absorbed in what you're doing.
- You look for no reward beyond that inherent in the activity itself.
- You possess great inner clarity. You know in every moment what to do, and you know immediately whether you've done it right or not.
- You know that your skills can meet the challenges of a situation, not that they are less than the situation demands, in which case you feel anxious, or more, in which case you are bored.
- You are serene. You forget your problems, expanding beyond your ego's bounds.
- Time speeds up. Hours seem like minutes.

Csikszentmihalyi's research indicates that 15 percent of us have never had the flow experience and that another 17 to 20 percent have it every day. The rest fall in between.

Of course a certain amount of love or money will help us to achieve a measure of contentment. But in Csikszentmihalyi's well-researched thinking, happiness comes from mastering skills and then applying them to challenging tasks. High flow moments can happen whether you're line-dancing, interviewing, writing haiku, cooking beans or playing pick-up basketball.

The concept of the "flow experience" isn't new. In 1889, Edwin Diller Starbuck wrote *The Psychology of Religion*, a book that attracted the attention of William James. In a lecture that appears in James' *Varieties of Religious Expe-*

rience, James quotes Starbuck about the flow experience in an unlikely pair – athletes and religious converts:

"An athlete . . . sometimes awakens suddenly to an understanding of the fine points of the game and to a real enjoyment of it, just as the convert awakens to an appreciation of religion. If he keeps on engaging in the sport, there may come a day when all at once the game plays itself through him – when he loses himself in some great contest."

Just so, a musician may master technique so beautifully that he "becomes the instrument through which the music flows," Starbuck adds.

James, further applying these ideas to religious conversion, writes that there is "a conscious and voluntary way and an involuntary and unconscious way in which mental results may get accomplished." The "volitional type of conversion" is generally less interesting than "the self-surrender type." After the will has done all that it can to help a person reach God, "it seems that the very last step must be left to other forces and performed without the help of [the will's] activity."

Perhaps every piece of high-quality work the world has ever seen – including the work of yielding to God – is the product both of effort and of effortlessness. As I have written and rewritten this essay through the years, I have alternated between the two states. At times, everything disappears except my memories of an interview with Csikszentmihalyi, the sound of a clicking keyboard, the sight of words appearing, letter by letter, on the computer screen and a stream of reverie. As I use words to rope in all the meaning I can, the world drops away and I float. At other times, self-doubt crowds accusingly around every word and phrase, sentence and paragraph, and I am all fear and effort. These entirely different states both serve the writing.

It is wondrous that I can be so happy when, absorbed in a task, I am nearly all gone or, to use Starbuck's phrase, an "instrument through which the music flows." Perhaps in the moment when I am an instrument . . . when I and the world both seem to vanish . . . I experience God in his immanence. Otherwise, who is it that is being so happy at that moment when "I" am most absent?

11.

Jacob's Ladder

Your young men will see visions, your old men will dream dreams.

Acts 2: 17

At 27, Jerome – later St. Jerome – described an experience of God in which "there was so much light, such a radiance of glory in those who stood about Him, that I fell upon my face not daring to raise my eyes." In the vision, God accused Jerome of being a student of the philosopher Cicero, not a Christian. Afterward, Jerome took an oath before God not to "touch profane books." He ended his description of the vision by saying, "And all that was no mere illusion of sleep, one of those vain dreams which often deceive us."

Another famous Christian dream – Jacob's about the ladder to heaven – likewise suggests the hold dreams have on Christian imaginations.

But dreams are also suspect. Jerome himself linked dreams to witchcraft and superstition. Dreams, like mystical visions, seem to fascinate workaday Christians. And plenty of people, not just Christians, seem to have mystical dreams. Kelly Bulkeley, a visiting scholar at the Graduate Theological Union, said in 2009 that there were "sufficient data" to propose that about half the population (more women than men) has experienced "mystical dreams."

Dreaming, however, remains on the fringe of religious experience. One reason is the difficulty of communicating dreams, especially those of the mystical variety. People who try often wind up blathering and feeling foolish. William James, in a lecture titled "Mysticism" in *The Varieties of Religious Experience*, writes, "This incommunicableness of the transport is the keynote of all mysticism. Mystical truth exists for the individual who has the transport, but for no one else." In the second of two lectures on conversion, James labels religious dreams as one of several "automatisms" of consciousness, a category that includes "hypnagogic hallucinations" and "odd impulses" as well.

This brings me to the story I'm aching to tell despite the incommunicableness of the vision that is its climax. I have to confess that my decision to give Christianity another chance was partly (a small part, really) the result of an encounter in a dream with something very much like the God of the mystics. Years passed before I labeled the dream I am thinking of as a vision of God. At the time I had the dream, I was disinterested in God but highly interested in magic – specifically the magic of attempting to manipulate dreams and control what occurred during their unfolding.

•

My engagement with dreamwork started in 1978, when I read a pop paperback called *Creative Dreaming*. Author Pat Garfield surveyed approaches to dreams taken by various groups, Hindus, Native Americans and Malaysians among them. What hooked me was Garfield's suggestion that dreamers could dream answers to pressing life questions. The practice, called dream-incubation, reportedly occurred among the ancient Greeks, at the temple of Asklepios at Epidaurus. Visitors in search of healing dreams purportedly drank potent wine administered by temple priests and then lay down to sleep – and dream – on the temple floor, which happened to be crawling with serpents.

According to Garfield, no tedious journey to a sacred reptile house is necessary for a contemporary American to incubate a dream. That person needs only a notepad, pen and flashlight on the bedstand. First, you frame a question very simply (a practice called *phrase incubation*); then, drifting off to sleep, you repeat the phrase to yourself as near the brink of sleep as possible. One night, Garfield wrote, would come a dream so memorable that it was unmistakably the answer to your question.

I couldn't remember my dreams at all in those days. Smoking dope every day didn't help. You need every ounce of short-term memory you have if you're going to haul a lunker dream from the depths of sleep. So I put this question to my dreams: "Why don't I remember you?" One night came this dream:

My phone rings. I pick up the receiver, and my favorite uncle starts talking. As I listen, the voice changes and becomes unfamiliar. So does the tone, transforming from friendly and easygoing to jeering and accusatory. Finally, the voice says, "I've been thinking a lot about what you asked me. And . . . well . . . **what do you know about me***?!"*

I woke up startled, my heart racing. The caller was obviously a dreamworld heavy. I felt upbraided. In coming months, in an effort to know more about Mister Unconscious, I read everything about dreaming I could lay hands on. The more I read, the more voluminous my dreams became, multiplying like those water-bucket-carrying broomsticks Mickey Mouse fought against in the Disney version of *The Sorcerer's Apprentice*.

At that point I had been teaching a couple of basic composition courses for about seven years. I had managed to apply for more than a hundred teaching positions and gotten two interviews. What should I do for my life's work? I wondered. So I incubated the phrase *Show me doing work I'd enjoy*. I guess it was about the 10th night that I dreamed of sitting with an old reporter in a restaurant basement. As he interviewed the owner, I was to take notes. I sat, listening, notebook open, staring at a blank page, panicked. I didn't know what I should write down. When I woke up, I was sure I should go to journalism school to find out what to write down. Voila: my career.

•

The dream journal I started to keep in 1978 grew to an inch high stack of typewritten pages in less than a year. Before sleep, I recited a phrase over and over: *Tonight, after I dream, I wake up and write the dream down.* The results were magical: I'd sometimes write down four or five dreams a night. My yearning to remember them was intense, and I believe that such yearning is the secret to succeeding. "When the Guest is being searched for," a sage named Kabir wrote, "it is the intensity of the longing for the Guest that does all the work."

Some of those dreams contained the seeds for spiritual growth. Yet back then, I didn't think of dreams as pointing the way to a higher order of reality; I took them to be THE higher order, an end, not the means. They were the story of myself, told to me through the haze of sleep. (The notion that dreams are the expression of random firings of the brain's nerve cells hadn't yet emerged.) I became a dream evangelist; I would all but stop strangers on the street to tell them the Good News about Dreaming. That year, I collected dreams with as much discipline as I taught grammar, prompting my officemate to ask more than once whether I thought I might be taking all this a bit too seriously. *Are you getting enough sleep?* she asked. *Shouldn't you be careful with that stuff?*

If there were dangers in my new religion, I didn't recognize them. Instead, I tried to make the impulse to collect and recollect dreams communal. I formed a Dream Club. A few of us met once a month or so to read dreams aloud. They shouldn't be analyzed, I said, but appreciated as a kind of storytelling in which each club member would gradually be known through the stories and images in her dreams. A former football player at a small college in Nebraska, who'd been a helicopter door gunner in Vietnam, played the hero in several people's dreams. One of us, for example, had him throwing a Volkswagen from the bottom of a river to the bank.

Another club member started joking about a personification I had invented: Senor Dream, I had said, led us on our fantastic night journeys. My friend talked more and more about Senor Dream until he was diagnosed as bipolar.

Meanwhile, I worked on a set of self-commands about how I'd behave in dreams, which I distilled into phrases like this: *Tonight, I fly*. (Who doesn't love a flying dream?) Lying in bed, I studied my dream rules, hoping to remember them during dreams. Garfield had described the work of anthropologist Kilton Stewart, who described the Senoi peoples of Malaysia training their children to fight off dream attackers and, after overcoming them, to extract a gift from them.

(A few years later, I read that the Senoi had been fooling with Stewart. Later still I heard that the exaggerations of the Senoi dream ethos were Stewart's inventions. Oddly, none of that matters. It may be a placebo, but phrase incubation works.)

One of my dream rules was to ask dream enemies what they wanted. I'd been running away from gangs of dream kids for years. One night, with a bunch of kids on bicycles chasing me, I suddenly remembered what I was supposed to do. I turned to them and shouted, "What do you want?" They giggled. "We just wanted to show you your house, Mister," one said.

I said, "Which one is it?"

Hands pointed in every direction. We all laughed.

Then one said, "I don't imagine they get anyone better than you to give these houses to."

From another source, I learned about a method for becoming lucid in a dream. In lucid dreaming, you figure out that you're dreaming while you're doing it, at which point you have some degree of choice about what happens next.

I'd learned about lucid dreaming from one of Carlos Castenada's books about Don Juan. Don Juan was a sorcerer, a brujo, whom a lot of counterculture types, myself included, thought was real until *Esquire* magazine outed Castenada's creation as a hoax. In one tale, the narrator is taught to look for his hands while in a dream and, seeing them, realize he's dreaming. Hoax or not, I actually did this once. The unconscious can be highly suggestible.

But not always. When you train yourself to confront dream enemies, they may fight back with surprising vigor – or do something completely unexpected. Once, strolling through a dream zocalo in Mexico, I took someone walking beside me to be dangerous, so I buried a screwdriver in his back. He turned, looked at me and said, "You don't always have to *kill* dream enemies, you know." Then he walked on, the screwdriver, still in place, jostling gently.

•

When anyone asked me about my religious faith in those days, I called myself an agnostic. Yet I often dreamed of Christians or of churches in those days. Religious motifs emerged almost as soon as I made a commitment to remembering my dreams.

February 5, 1978. People are sleeping on the floor of a big room. A band of us are awake. We somehow know that the sleepers are Christians. Those of us who are awake are leaving on a trek into the mountains. There is a hint of danger – that the numbers of people like us are shrinking, and we may be hunted down.

March 5, 1979. A light comes on in a room, and I look in. I see a friend sitting with a couple of other people. They've been discussing my religious "problem." I tell my friend there's no problem. I've decided to be a Catholic. My friend thinks this is smarter than being an atheist.

Eventually, I tried to incubate a dream to answer the question *What do all these religious dreams mean?* Eventually I dreamed the magical dream I'm about to describe, which I take to be, even now, the most visionary experience, awake or asleep, of my life.

I walk into the living room of the house where I grew up.

I approach a north-facing window. I stand there, light streaming in. It's unlike any earthly light that I've encountered. This light is more than merely physical, more than a cascade of photons. This is a spiritual light (a label I don't apply to it until I wake). At the moment that I am standing in the light, it floods me with joy bred of a certainty: I AM LOVED. Overwhelmed, something knotted and resistant inside of me dissolves. Tears run down my face.

I awaken, near tears, thinking that God ***was*** that light or somehow the light contained God.

A few nights later, I dreamed this: *I walk into the kitchen of the house where I grew up. I stand by the screen door. I look down the alley that runs behind our house. The mesh of the screen obscures my view, so I swing the door open and step onto the porch to get a better look. The screen is still there before my eyes. There must be screen embedded in my glasses, I think. Strange.*

I take off the glasses.

But the screen is still there.

Is the screen in my eyes? In my brain? Suddenly, aware that I'm dreaming, I feel playful. I step forward, plant my hands on the porch railing, flip over it and fall gently toward the brick backyard.

Sometimes, in a lucid dream, you fly. That night I found that a slow fall can be just as much fun.

•

For a long time, I thought the dreams of the light and of the screen door had occurred the same night. Maybe I fused them because they are both about vision, or because they both feel numinous – what C.G. Jung called "big dreams." I hope some day to be visited by an experience as powerful as that of the light, but in a waking state. I really haven't paid much attention to dreams in the past 20 years. Religion as a source of vision is less important to me now than is religion as force for creating a community that serves.

I recently asked an agnostic intellectual I know whether, if she had a choice to experience a religious vision, she'd even want it – given that the experience might act as a barrier between her and some of her friends. At first she said yes, then backpedaled. "That's an interesting question," she said.

I understood her hesitancy. Who wants to be the object of whispers about being a "religious nut"? Not me: The morning after my dream of light, I wrote in my journal that it was "nearly a religious experience." Today, I think, *C'mon, Roger. Religious experiences don't admit of degrees, do they? Whaddya mean* ***NEARLY*** *a religious experience?*

I'm not surprised that I fudged. After all, vision comes at a cost. It doesn't just expand your world. The resulting certainty can also narrow it.

12.

'The Market Is God'

I'd rather be a Mennonite than a Mammonite.

Anon.

God moves in mysterious ways. So does the Dow Jones Industrial Average. That's why some who wouldn't be caught dead thumbing through the Holy Bible, the Talmud or the Koran will treat the *Value Line Investment Survey* or *Morningstar* reports as if they were holy writ. Einstein said this about mystery: "It is the fundamental emotion which stands at the cradle of true art and true science." A sense of mystery and wonder also can be found at the bottom of religion and investing – and if people can't access that sense in one domain, they may seek it in the other.

I know about the mysteries of investing because I became fervent about it in 1995 and 1996, when I produced an unpublished manuscript about the stock market. My idea was to keep a log that would record my experience in the first year of buying common stocks – not just the vanilla-flavored mutual funds that I'd been plunking money into for years. Writing the book pressed me to read piles of financial books, magazines and newspapers, and that's when I learned that for some people, the stock market is a surrogate for God.

Not an original thought. Many others have also sensed the parallels, and rivalries, between religion and entrepreneurship (aka "God" and "Mammon"). In March 1999, an *Atlantic Monthly* piece by Harvard theologian Harvey Cox was headlined "The Market as God." Cox wasn't just writing about the stock market, but about marketing-mindedness run amok. He wrote, "There lies embedded in the business pages an entire theology, which is comparable in scope if not in profundity to that of Thomas Aquinas or Karl Barth."

Some of the investors who worship at the Church of the Almighty Dollar are fundamentalists, their faith containing a Manichean twist. Just as evangelical Christians love God and fear the dark force personified by Satan, these investors love the Bull and dread the Bear. Yet for both fundamentalist Christians and investors, it's not always clear when you're in bad company. Satan is famous for his disguises and treacheries, while bear markets are notorious for looking like mere corrections, temporary downturns in an otherwise upwardly bound market. By giving that appearance, bear markets tempt greedy investors into buying stock at the wrong moment. Discerning the work of God from that of the Devil is important to the religious fundamentalist; discerning whether you're in a bull market or a bear market is important to the pocketbook of the marketplace Manichean.

To navigate these uncertain waters, both Christians and investors cling to articles of faith. As a child, I recited the Apostles' Creed every Sunday. "I believe in God the Father Almighty, maker of heaven and earth," it began, "and in Jesus Christ, his only begotten Son, our Lord." If I were to put words to an Investor's Creed it might be this: "I believe in long-term investing – a buy-and-hold philosophy – and in dollar-cost-averaging." According to this mainline creed, wise investors buy stocks or funds and hold on to them through thick and thin because, given enough time, the market will rise again. Dollar cost averaging means tithing a fixed percentage of earnings from every paycheck to the market. Both strategies lower the risk of being fooled by bears and bulls.

Roger Lowenstein, writing for the *Wall Street Journal* in September 1996, gave an example of an investor who had this faith. Lowenstein's metaphors were perfect: "Forget, for the moment, the splinter denominations, where evangelists and faith healers profess devotion to certain stocks, fads, nostrums and technologies at any price. In the main chapel, there are a goodly number of old-fashioned practitioners like Joe Smith. A marketing manager at a unit of Harsco Corp., he has been stashing money away, beginning with $10 a month, since the late 1960s. Mr. Smith preaches the gospel of long-term investing."

Love God with all your heart, soul and mind and love your neighbor as yourself seems to me to be the heart of Jesus' teaching. The heart of the market's wisdom? "Buy low, sell high." Sometimes a banker is credited with this apothegm, saying that he'd become wealthy by buying "sheep" and selling "deer." However, I suspect the words probably tumbled from the lips of some W.C. Fieldslike cynic of a broker at lunch one day with his pals. They imply an ease where none exists.

•

Besides proverbial wisdom, investors, like other spiritual folk, also have gospels and gurus, though they're more transient than Matthew, Mark, Luke and John, Moses or John the Baptist. Benjamin Graham and David Dodd's *Security Analysis*, which counsels investors in methods for identifying companies whose stock is undervalued, represents the spirit of the age when it was written: the Great Depression. On the other hand, the *oeuvre* of former Fidelity Magellan mutual fund guru Peter Lynch is biased toward investment in young companies that are in a growth burst, a nice match with the go-go spirit of America in the 1980s.

The turnover in market gurus is high. In the mid-'90s, the perception by investors of Jeff Vinik, then manager of the Fidelity Magellan fund, underwent a huge correction. In early 1996, because of the size of that fund and its influence on the returns of various stocks, his moves were, like God's, both mysterious and the subject of speculation. But that was the year that Vinik lost faith in stocks, plunging his fund's cash reserves into bonds. His returns paled and media gave him the hook. Goldman Sachs' Abby Joseph Cohen, who kept the faith that the long-running bull market of the 1990s would continue, took his mantle.

All in all, near the end of the 20th century, investing was the only way some people could tap into awe, humility, dread and other staples of the "spiritual" experience. John Rothchild, a ghostwriter for Lynch and a self-described failed investor in the book *A Fool and His Money*, quotes a corn trader on the commodities exchange:

". . . He had some rather negative things to say, which I wrote down as follows:

'When I first came down here, I was Mr. Big Ego. I had a law degree and here were all these ex-cops and truck drivers and people with 200-word vocabularies trading in the pits. I figured I'd make a killing, right? With this competition, how could you lose? Then I get the shit kicked out of me. . . . You know what I've learned down here? Humility. Discipline. You come into this business with any sense of superiority, and you're dead.

'Sooner or later, you find out who you are. That's what this game is about, finding out who you are. People say the market's this or the market's that, and they begin to think they can understand it. They discover they're wrong. They can't understand it. The market is . . . the market is God.'"

That corn trader speaks for many investors, humbled or otherwise.

•

Because of the parallels between the domains of the spirit and of the market, they're destined to be rivals. "Ye cannot serve God and Mammon," warned St. Jerome. After all, how can a rich man attain heaven? With a lot more stress and strain than it takes a camel to pass through the eye of a needle. One issue is that the role of money in a human life is defined in radically different ways by the spiritual and secular worlds.

My Christian mother was careful to remind me, when I misquoted the Bible to her, that it wasn't money that's the root of all evil but the love of it. No one argues against its utility, least of all those who have to pay pastors, buy bricks-and-mortar, fund charities and missions. A Calvinist strain even points to the accrual of wealth as proof of human virtue and divine election. In an investment classic titled *The Money Game*, writer "Adam Smith" (a pseudonym) quotes a Bishop Lawrence as having said, "In the long run, it is only to the man of morality that wealth comes. Godliness is in league with riches. Material prosperity makes the national character sweeter, more Christlike." Sometimes the church has been more crass about money, as when Johann Tetzel jacked up the price of indulgences in the 16th century, pitching his case in rhyme: "When the coin into the platter pings, the soul out of purgatory springs."

Nevertheless, Christians generally sense the threat to Christianity of wealth's being idolized (in principle, if not in practice). When great wealth is accrued through hard work, it may inflate the ego and diminish the value of God's grace. Cox, in the *Atlantic Monthly* piece, notes that many are threatened by the world's idolatry of wealth, not just Christians: "I am beginning to think that for all the religions of the world, however they may differ from one another, the religion of The Market has become the most formidable rival, the more so because it is rarely recognized as religion."

The difference of the spiritual and business communities regarding money derives to an extent from definitions of community. Denominations and churches may quarrel and splinter, but they sense that God would prefer that they cooperate. The market, on the other hand, identifies independent self-sufficiency with virtue. The power of wealth to isolate was a theme of the late Joseph Campbell in an interview with Bill Moyers for the PBS series *The Power of Myth*. Speaking of dragons, Campbell said, "Our Western dragons represent greed. The Chinese dragon is different. It represents the vitality of the swamps and comes up beating its belly and bellowing, 'Haw ha ha haww.' That's a lovely kind of dragon, one that yields the bounty of the waters, a great, glorious gift. But the dragon of our Western tales tries to collect and keep everything to himself. In his secret cave he guards things: heaps of gold and perhaps a captured virgin. He doesn't know what to do with either, so he just guards and keeps."

The irony is that hoarding the gold can be dangerous even to the big dragons. John Kenneth Galbraith, writing in *The Great Crash: 1929*, talks about a "bad distribution of wealth" as one of a handful of causes of the Great Depression. About 5 percent of the population with the highest incomes in 1929 received about a third of all personal income, Galbraith estimates. The country's economic well-being depended on the rich spending more robustly than they possibly could: "[They] cannot buy great quantities of bread," Galbraith writes. Yet it is upon the buying of bread and other equally humble goods – not the amassing of wealth in caves – that the stock market and the big dragons depend. Moreover, sharing these goods makes community. The earliest Christian groups knew that. Acts 2 notes that "the faithful all lived together and owned everything in common; they sold their goods and possessions and shared out the proceeds among themselves according to what each one needed."

•

I found in my year of intense focus on the market that although stocks are often called "securities," there is little about owning stocks that confers security. Of course, God's ways and our world aren't predictable either. The randomness of world affairs challenges the spiritual person for the same reason that the random rambling of stock prices upsets the studious investor. The difference is that the spiritual person is asked to embrace ignorance and powerlessness, to welcome adversity and to cultivate the art of surrender – to put up with disappointment and puzzlement and not be paralyzed. The basis for this is an assumption of God's love, despite all riddles and mystery. If five loaves and two fishes could feed a multitude, it wasn't because they were wisely invested by a keen-eyed savior who timed the market perfectly and got an explosive return. Instead, the story goes, they were blessed by an immoderately loving God who provides bounty without regard to our effort or ability. That love let a few loaves and fishes feed many. Trusting in that love runs contrary to common sense.

Even harder to integrate is an idea correlated to that of God's bounty: that "ownership" is largely an illusion. In the *Screwtape Letters*, by C.S. Lewis, the devil Screwtape tells his student Wormwood that a "sense of ownership [in humans] in general is always to be encouraged," because it serves the dark forces. People who own a pair of boots and express this relationship in the phrase "my boots" will also use phrases like "my dog," "my wife," "my country" and "my God." In using such language, people forget that power over one's boots is a different affair than control of a dog, a spouse or God. They forget the limits of their authority.

I have found it enlightening to "own" 78 acres of Kansas countryside. When I try to call the woods and fields, the sycamores and hickories, the creeks and terraces "mine," it feels delusional. All I really "own" is an ability to walk on those acres without asking permission. And I don't own that either without a small contingency: that it can all end suddenly if a chunk of plaque breaks loose in an artery. In our dreams, we may want to be dragons who own virgins, but the reality is that we're more like lilies of the field. Our sense of agency and of ownership is an illusion. Our world is on temporary loan.

Separate Magisteria

The net of science covers the empirical universe: what is it made of (fact) and why does it work this way (theory). The net of religion extends over questions of moral meaning and value. These two magisteria do not overlap, nor do they encompass all inquiry (consider, for starters, the magisterium of art and the meaning of beauty). . . . I believe, with all my heart, in a respectful, even loving concordat between our magisteria.

Stephen Jay Gould
"Nonoverlapping Magisteria"
Natural History

13.

Your Brain on God

During the epiphany, I knew what it was like to have a mind without ego, a benign awareness of things near and far and an absence of the familiar worries. Rather than my being the one doing the seeing, thinking or feeling, I felt, ever so briefly, seen-through, thought-through and felt-through. It was as if I were given a chance that morning to experience my life from God's perspective, seeing it in relation to other lives in other times and places, sensing the ease of it, the sheer luck of it. This happened in an unlikely setting. I was sitting on the toilet, staring at a fat roll of toilet paper freshly installed in the chrome dispenser.

I'd been reading *Poisonwood Bible*, by Barbara Kingsolver. The book draws a picture of village life in Africa vivid enough to make me certain I never want to step foot into an African village. Almost everyone in Kilanga has been maimed. They're all missing digits or limbs or teeth. Hunger is pervasive, its edge blunted only by manioc cooked into a glop. The driver ants, capable of picking a chicken clean in minutes, are not even the worst news about the place. A green mamba takes that honor.

Because of Kingsolver's book, I had begun the day of my toilet-paper vision thinking about starving children whose bellies balloon because their abdominal muscles are weak from want of protein. And then, looking at the toilet paper, I *really* saw it. White, fluffy, soft . . . it wasn't just *any* roll. It signaled my life's bounty, my extraordinary privilege. The white noise of cooled air pouring through the floor vent was a cushion lifting me heavenward. It was only 7:30 a.m., but the Kansas heat and humidity were oppressive; here it was delightfully cool. The showerhead – well, it made me happy to look at. I felt blessed that in the garage was a reliable car and in the kitchen a cereal that provides me with 100 percent of the minimum daily requirement of 12 vitamins and minerals. Just who was this person noticing the gift of my usually taken-for-granted life? Couldn't be me . . . and yet it was.

I turned my head and stared at a family photograph. There was my grandfather, Albert Katterjohn, handsome and young, standing beside his German brothers and sisters. Seated in the foreground were his stern-looking, wide-jawed hausfrau mother and his bearded, dewy-eyed dad. I thought about all the German DNA (and industry and bull-headedness and smugness) I'm packing. Of course, like most of my fellow Americans, I'm no purebred. We are a nation of mutts crossbred of chromosomes and ancestries to reach the improbable singularity of our lives, and I sensed the skein of communities, copulations and sheer accidents required to deposit me on this planet, in this land, in this house, on this morning having this once-and-only-once (not in broad outline but in terms of its constellation of details) revelation.

I thought about all the other objects in the house connecting me to other lives. The weeping Buddha on the mantle, from Thailand, was given me by friends George and AnnMarie; the watercolor images of shiny black doorknobs and silver spoons were painted by my first wife; an oak coffee table was the product of my father's handicraft, as was the lamp he'd carved, in the shape of an Easter Island-like face, from a bowling pin.

Was the effect of this cascade of thought, this seizure of peace, God's work? Or was it the result of slowed firing in the parietal region of my brain? Of increased activity in the limbic system? A surge of dopamine?

•

One day at a brain bank, I watched as the director sliced a brain. The first pieces looked like cauliflower cut in cross-section.

"Those of us who study the brain," he said, "become obsessed by it."

Why? I asked.

Because, he said, it's 3 percent of our body weight but uses 15 percent of all the calories burned by the body.

Because, he said, of all the proteins our bodies manufacture, about 30 percent are brain proteins.

Because, he said, to produce a full set of nerve cells for the brain, a growing fetus must produce an average of 50,000 nerve cells *a minute.* The theory goes that we make four times more than we ever use, then destroy all but the finest.

Because, he said, the brain is the only tissue in creation that has a sense of mortality and a vision of God.

•

An entire field of study has sprung up concerning where visions and epiphanies are sensed within the three-pound gelatinous organ encased in skull. The field is called neurotheology, and earlier in this century it was the subject of books like *Why God Won't Go Away,* by Drs. Andrew Newberg and Eugene D'Aquili, the *Principles of Neurotheology* (Newberg again) and magazine cover stories.

Scientific studies of the perception of God are fascinating, in part, because of the different uses to which they are put by believers and non-believers. To believers, they evidence a possibility that God has engineered into the brain a capacity to know the divine; disbelievers use the same information to provide a materialist explanation for some of the feelings that religion and spirituality engender, in effect saying, *This God stuff is just the product of brain chemistry, pal.*

A few brain areas have earned special attention from those who study the relationship of nerve cells and the Almighty.

The first, the parietal lobe, is found near the crown of the head, just a bit past halfway back. Deeper in the brain and more toward the front is the temporal lobe. The temporal lobe is one of several structures within the limbic system, which seems in general to be implicated in spiritual feelings.

The parietal lobe is the brain's orientation-awareness center. Our sense that we are who we are, and everything else is not us (the opposite of my relational sense of reality on the morning of my epiphany) is an endowment of the parietal lobe. Newberg has discovered that with the onset of deep meditative states – whether those are Buddhist or Catholic, whether they are induced in silence or by repetitive chanting – nerve-cell firing slows way down in the parietal lobe.

In a 2001 issue of *Newsweek*, senior editor Sharon Begley wrote about a woman named Sister Celeste, noting that "during [her] most intensely religious moments, when she felt a palpable sense of God's presence and an absorption of her self into his being, her brain displayed changes like those in . . . Tibetan Buddhist meditators: her orientation area [the parietal lobe] went dark."

Some religious experiences may have a negative effect on the brain. A study reported in 2011, for example, indicated that over the long haul, a portion of the brain called the hippocampus may be negatively affected by "born-again" experiences. Duke University researchers reported that a group of believers who had experienced "life-changing" religious awakenings also showed some shrinking of the hippocampus region later in life: "Greater hippocampal atrophy was observed longitudinally in this study among born-again Protestants, Catholics, and those reporting no religious affiliation, compared with non born-again Protestants. These findings may reflect potential cumulative stress associated with being a member of a religious minority." Atrophy in this region of the brain is problematic because it's been a marker of late life mental health problems, including depression and dementia.

•

A very different brain area, the temporal lobe, appears to mediate a different kind of religious ecstasy: extremely vivid visions such as those experienced by St. Theresa of Avila. V.S. Ramachandran, in his book *Phantoms in the Brain*, co-written with Sandra Blakeslee, describes the experiments of a Canadian psychologist, Michael Persinger. Persinger stimulated parts of his own temporal lobe and experienced God for the first time in his life. To Ramachandran, a professor at the University of California at San Diego, this was no surprise:

"Every medical student is taught that patients with epileptic seizures originating in [the left temporal lobe] can have intense, spiritual experiences during the seizures and sometimes become preoccupied with religious and moral issues even during the seizure-free . . . periods."

Some acquire what neurologists call "temporal lobe personality": a tendency to see cosmic significance in trivial events, to be humorless, to be self-important and to maintain elaborate diaries containing, among other things, mystical symbols and notations – a trait labeled hypergraphia.

Ramachandran once experimented with two volunteers who had temporal lobe personality. First, electrodes were attached to their hands to measure their galvanic skin response to various stimuli.

"Once settled in front of a computer screen, they were shown random samples of several types of words and images," Ramachandran writes. There were words for commonplace objects like shoes; familiar faces of family members; unfamiliar faces; sexually arousing words and pictures; four-letter words involving sex, extreme violence and horror (an alligator eating a person alive, for example); and religious icons and words.

Most people given this test show huge responses to sexy or violent pictures or sexy words. A fairly large number respond to familiar faces. Most show little or no response to anything else.

"To our amazement what we found in the two patients tested was a heightened response mainly to religious words and icons," Ramachandran writes. "Their response to the other categories, including sexual words and images, which ordinarily evoke a powerful response, was strangely diminished compared to what is seen in normal individuals."

The limbic system, within which the temporal lobe is lodged, is the starting point for other sorts of woo-woo experiences. Stimulated here and there, the result can be dreamlike hallucinations, out-of-body sensations or feelings of déjà vu. According to Newberg, because of its involvement in religious and spiritual experiences, the limbic system has sometimes been referred to as the "transmitter to God."

Newberg takes no sides when it comes to the contrary claims of science and spirituality in regard to God and the brain. He notes that the "neurological realness" of a sense of oneness "is by no means proof of an absolute spiritual reality. . . . On the other hand, by explaining mystical experience as a neurological function, we do not intend to suggest that it can't be something more. What we do suggest is that scientific research supports the possibility that a mind can exist without ego, that awareness can exist without self."

•

My toilet paper epiphany was not of the Pauline kind. It was, instead, a peaceful and powerful experience of connection. I sensed the abundance of my own life and felt in it the presence of other lives, fictional, living and long-gone. I experienced my ancestors as I never had, loving them almost impersonally, as vessels of a life force that keeps rolling and tumbling through time and space. Best of all, the usual cacophony of quarrelsome interior voices and competing impulses ceased.

When I try to map the experience against what I know about the brain, I suspect the firing in my pariental lobe must have slowed that morning. It makes me glad that science is establishing the neurological bases of some aspects of the spiritual life, because, for me, such explanations make it easier for me to admit experiences like these into conversation. It's also true that the peace I felt that morning surpassed in importance any explanation of its cause.

Begley said in an online chat after her *Newsweek* article came out, "Only a third or so of Americans say they've had a spiritual experience . . . but more than 90 percent say they believe in God."

I suppose I should be elated to be part of the 33 percent. But I'm greedy; the epiphany just wet my whistle. So far, though, God shows no sign of wanting to quench that thirst. Have you heard the phrase "faith work"? It comes to mind here because for some of us faith is not a gift left on our doorstep (or, if it is, it may arrive scrawny and crying). It has been this way for me, except for the rare morning of my toilet-paper vision and a few other numinous moments. And so I've tried to nourish this orphan with prayer, study and service, hoping it will flourish as we trudge across arid miles of doubt looking for oases of vision either graced upon, or invented by, the only tissue in creation that has a sense of mortality and a vision of God.

14.

Life Is Just a Four-Letter Word

I and 10 other journalists were at a weeklong biochemistry program at the Marine Biological Laboratory in Woods Hole, Massachusetts, designed to give us a hands-on experience of science. One of our teachers, a biologist from Northwestern, said that our week in the laboratory might lead us to a religious experience. I snapped to attention and asked the scientist for details.

He smiled and said, "Over a beer, maybe."

Our class gave us an experience of science that was sterilized and scrubbed of risk. The experiment we conducted was so carefully rigged by our professors and their assistants that a pack of baboons would have had eureka experiences that week. I'm grateful for all the legwork the lab assistants performed in advance of our arriving at class because otherwise I would have been chewing up pipettes from fear and frustration. As it was, pairs of journalists – my lab partner was a freelancer named Ken – were scientific big-game hunters led directly to their prey.

The climax of the week for me and Ken was sprinkling some kind of chemical on a slip of paper. Tidy blue marks magically appeared, indicating the presence of proteins of a certain molecular weight.

A scientist hurried over. "Great job," he said, "you got it!"

We beamed. Now we had to rinse the paper with water to fix those blue marks. I nabbed a squirt bottle off a countertop. Ken was the brains of the outfit, the rigor – the piano builder, let's say. I was the brawn, the slop in the system – the roofer. Ken was the guy who kept the immaculate lab notes so my only work was gathering English-majorish impressions. I ran up to Ken with the squirt bottle. Here ya go, boss. He splashed liquid into the dish.

Then: "What's HAPPENING?!" He sounded like a mother whose baby had rolled off the dock.

The slip of paper was curdling. I'd never seen paper do that. We turned the squirt bottle around. Where the word "water" should have appeared was, instead, the vile word "methanol." We'd sauced the paper with alcohol, not H2O.

Sorry, Ken.

I learned that week to admire the patience, precision, rigor and fortitude of cell biologists. For them, the devil's in such details as dropped slides and stray bubbles and grabbing the right squeeze bottle. A blown detail can undo hours, days or weeks of work. I was gladder than ever that I'm a journalist, which is bash-and-fit work, not a piano builder. But another lesson from that week was more profound.

•

The first thing we did during the workshop was watch, on a video monitor, the cells of clam eggs divide. The chief players in this drama were spidery-looking filaments and white specks. The scientists said the specks were chromosomes. I wrote that down. If they'd told me the specks were pixilated angels, I would have written that down. When it comes to science, I'm a pushover.

We spent a few days discovering one of the proteins within the spidery-looking filaments. We pushed onward, into still tinier kingdoms, finding the gene that's responsible for making that protein and then trying to determine the order of the chemical building blocks that make up the gene.

The building blocks of genes are called nucleotides. There are four kinds, and they are as basic to a biologist as north, south, east and west is to a navigator; as Matthew, Mark, Luke and John are to a preacher; as sensation, emotion, intuition and judgment were to C.G. Jung. The nucleotides are adenine, cytosine, guanine and thymine. We'll call them a, c, g and t, OK? In illustrations of a spiraling double helix of DNA, the nucleotides are represented as horizontal rungs that hold together the vertical strands. A single strand of DNA comprises about 3 billion a's, c's, g's and t's. This stuff is a miracle of compaction. If you split open a cell and unkinked a folded-up, twisted-up, wadded-up strand of DNA and hung it on a clothesline to dry, it'd be about a yard long.

Before I nuked our experiment, Ken and I had discovered a fairly long sequence of a's, c's, g's and t's in the gene we were stalking. Not its entire alphabetic string, mind you, but a good healthy run of 187 letters. That was just a fragment of the gene's whole sequence – but it was more than enough to identify the gene.

At a website database maintained by the National Center for Biotechnology Information, we typed in our 187 letters.

And that's when I had the religious feelings the scientist from Northwestern had hinted at.

I knew that cells of many different life forms are much alike. As science writer Boyce Rensberger says in his book *Life Itself*, "A human brain cell . . . is not more complicated than a one-celled creature inhabiting pond scum." During our computer search, we found that our 187-letter string of nucleotides shows up, almost wholly intact, in various creatures – clams, fruit flies, yeasts, slime molds, octopuses, me and Ken. Biologists explain this by saying that some genes are "highly conserved" from species to species. They mean that evolution, often praised for introducing new wrinkles into creation, can also be a real lazybones. It hangs on to some genes for eons and sprinkles them liberally among species.

The words "highly conserved" do no justice to the sense of magic I experienced as I gawked at the computer screen and understood my fellowship with slime molds and yeasts. I suddenly felt more linked to all my fellow earthlings, even scientists.

That afternoon, our class cruised some coves on a collecting vessel. Crew members dredged the waters to show us squirmy things that live there. At one point I lifted a jar of captured life to the sky. Larval crabs darted through the brine, and jellyfish smaller than thimbles heaved in slow pulses.

The fact that life – yours, mine, a sponge's or an anteater's – rests on four chemical pillars and the endless grunt work of cells didn't seem to me to trivialize our existence.

It made Earth homier.

15.

The Beginning of Everything

Adrian Melott, a roly-poly astrophysicist and hairy-all-over man, was wearing a sleeveless tie-dye T-shirt that day at the gym when he told me that, strolling through K-Mart one day, he'd spotted a table piled high with copies of a book, written for second graders, recounting the Genesis story.

"Only $4.95," he joked. "A real bargain."

Then he went online looking for a book for kids that told the creation story that scientists believe, starring the Big Bang. The search proved fruitless. He said, "The best I've done on the Big Bang are books at the 5th or 6th grade level. It'll get mentioned in a book on space, say. It's the same with evolution."

He thinks publishers may be afraid of Creationists. I think it likelier that publishers are afraid they'll wind up with a book that has to be remaindered. Eventually he self-published a storybook titled *How We Happened: The Beginning of Everything*, targeted at fourth and fifth graders.

Melott's book starts with a bang, the Big Bang, that ferocious explosion of a superdense speck of matter billions of years ago that sent particles spraying in all directions at speeds much higher than those at which light travels, producing a universe that's still rocketing outward across the face of the void. The particles were pretty evenly distributed, with the exception of some lumps here and there. Gravity shaped the lumps into clouds. The clouds whirled 'round and 'round, and suns blinked on in the middle of some of the clouds. Then planets formed. And so the universe grew, endowed with a structure like that of a sea sponge, Melott says. Superclusters of galaxies containing a mass of 10 million billion suns form great walls, and in between them are enormous voids.

Got that? OK, but do you buy it? Do **you** really, personally believe that the universe was wrought from the explosion of a tiny chunk of matter? Cosmologists do – and so do I – even though it hardly seems true even if it DID happen and IS still happening. The scenario makes me feel like asking a bunch of smart-aleck questions.

And what was going on before the explosion?

And why'd the marble explode?

And why did it explode in all directions? Why didn't it just split a side? In which case you'd have a split screen universe, with all the stuff on one side and a Great Big Nothing on the other?

Of course other cosmological theories are far weirder than the Big Bang. Consider the dream of a University of California at Berkeley cosmologist named Andre Linde. Linde says our universe may be just one bubble in a foam of universes, with each universe governed by different laws of physics. Believing in God seems less fanciful when compared with ideas like that.

Now of course scientists like Melott are careful to point out a distinction between spiritual and scientific ideas: Cosmological theories are evidence-based, and, therefore, aren't at all like the stories you read in the Bible. So what's the evidence for the Big Bang? First, scientists say that data tell them that everything is flying away from everything else and in all directions. So if you run the movie backwards, what you find is that tiny speck of matter.

Moreover, the Big Bang theory, formulated in the 1940s, has helped make several accurate predictions – and to scientists, the power of a theory to make predictions is a show of strength. For example, the Big Bang theory predicted the temperature of certain electromagnetic radiation, the so-called cosmic microwave background, that's way, way, way, way out there. Its temperature is now known to four decimal places: 2.7135 degrees Kelvin. Give or take. On your home thermometer that's a chilly 450 degrees below zero. The Big Bang theorists also predicted that the universe would turn out to be about three-quarters hydrogen by weight and one-quarter helium, with just a smidge of everything else. Bingo. They got it.

The trouble with the really far-out ideas, like Linde's, is that they're more mathematical than anything else. I can't tell you how equations can be translated into bubble universes – I got thrown off the math train for good in the second week of high-school calculus. An alternate way of explaining the problem with Linde's ideas is to note that nobody can think of an experiment to prove the existence of bubble universes. In the experimental sense, the Big Bang theory is solid, but some late-breaking cosmological ideas, the kind that *Time* and *Newsweek* feature, have about them the odor of faith, not science.

•

Let me go back to the question that always troubles me, though, when I hear about the Big Bang: Could anything have existed before it? A few years ago, Leon Lederman, director emeritus of Fermilab National Accelerator Laboratory, said that maybe the laws of physics existed before the universe. But if someone asks him how the laws got there, Lederman says, "Go across the street to the theology school, and ask those guys, because I don't know."

I'd agree with Lederman that theology and cosmology aren't on the same block – but they do strike me as being in the same neighborhood. For example, both Christianity and physics are haunted by paradox. The belief that Jesus Christ was both man and God, for example, is on a par with the idea that an electron is both a particle and a wave (until you observe it, when, presto, it becomes one or the other). The idea that the visible world of the senses follows Newton's laws and that the atomic world follows the far weirder laws of quantum mechanics is about as hard to digest as the Christian notion that reality comprises both an earthly and a spiritual realm.

Both religion and physics engender a sense of wonder. Religion has miraculous spiritual healings, such as the disappearance of a 12-inch-long spinal tumor following a religious vision reported by Reynolds Price in his book *A Whole New Life*. Science has miraculous facts that defy common sense. The emptiness of atoms is one that stuns me. The nucleus is by far the most massive part of an atom, yet, even so, the nucleus occupies only one ten-millionth of the atom's total volume. That is, atoms are astonishingly empty affairs.

What does that say about the rest of the "known" world?

Christianity and physics also share an interest in the beginning and end of things. It used to be that both believed the end would be dramatic. With religion, you got the second coming, the sheep separated from the goats. With physics, at least physics until the 1990s, there were dreams of a final Big Crunch, a matter smashup at the end of time as a result of gravity's pulling everything back together again. Then, alas, evidence arose that though the expansion of the universe was slowing, it probably wasn't slowing enough to generate a Big Crunch. Instead, it's likely that there'll be a big chill. Just as a can of hairspray gets cold as it empties, because the gas inside spreads out, so will our universe get colder and colder – and for the very same reason.

•

Toward the end of the millennium, the possibility of a rapprochement between science and religion was big news. There was a major article in the *New York Times* and a *Newsweek* cover story. Spurring the coverage was a conference in California, titled "Science and the Spiritual Quest," that brought together scientists, most of them Christians, Jews or Muslims. The money behind the event came from the John Templeton Foundation. Templeton is a Wall Street legend, a global investor who was known for beginning his mutual fund company's annual meetings with a prayer. Maybe it was a sign of Millennium Fever that an investment wizard wanted to find a way for science and religion to be comfortable (if odd) bedfellows.

But science and religion can coexist, I think, so long as there's tolerance. In Melott's own life, science and religion have gotten along OK. He was first a physics major, then a Unitarian minister for seven years and is now a physics professor. I asked him about his personal beliefs. He said, "All I know for sure is that there's a universe here that allows things to evolve and develop purpose – including love."

I said, "You mean, for example, that we humans can develop a sense of purpose, a mission in life. And that all of life has the purpose of trying to stay alive?"

He said, "That's right. That's all I know for sure."

"Is that enough for you?"

"I guess so. I don't think I long for more."

He's less into reconciling science and religion than into according a place to each. The power of science, he says, is to produce what he calls "true myths" that are both magical and – unlike the myths of religious faith – verifiable.

Melott thinks that one of science's magical ideas is the fact that *everything* – animal, vegetable or mineral – is constructed from the residue of exploded stars. "That's the magic of how we are made and the truth," he writes in a document prepared for Unitarians to read. "It's testable and has as much magical power as any Native American story of birth, of creation." Melott believes that religion should build on and around these "true myths" of science – the Big Bang, evolution, the ubiquity of stardust and on and on. "My main thing is that you don't need to lie about science to make it magical," he said. "You have solar flares – fountains of flames larger than the Earth. You have black holes and nuclear energy. Why do you need pyramid power?"

I tell him the trouble is that you can't make a religion of solar flares and black holes alone. You need more than something awesome, because awe isn't personal enough. Lots of people, I say, want to believe in a God who loves them personally enough to answer prayer – or at least take requests. Who has a plan for their lives. Who is the reason that "everything happens for a reason," as they say. Science doesn't offer a universe whose beating heart is love, or in which love much matters except as a manifestation of oxytocin, dopamine or some other hormone or neurotransmitter – or as the driving wheel of evolution.

One last thought. No matter how much the heart yearns for science and religion to be reconciled, "the uncomfortable truth is that the two beliefs [in the gods and in biology] are not factually compatible," writes E.O. Wilson, emeritus professor of biology at Harvard, in his book *Consilience: The Unity of Knowledge*. "As a result, those who hunger for both intellectual and religious truth will never completely achieve both."

Wilson, who once called himself a "reborn evangelical," takes a separate-but-equal approach to science and religion. He writes that science, through the centuries, has taken us farther and farther from a personal God. "The spirits our ancestors knew intimately first fled the rocks and trees, then the distant mountains. Now they are in the stars, where their final extinction is possible. *But we cannot live without them.* [Emphasis is Wilson's.] People need a sacred narrative." Wilson calls for "mutual respect" between science and religion.

I second the motion. Jihads by the religious right against evolution or sneers from intellectuals about spiritual-minded clucks exhaust me. What's the point of setting up straw men by choosing extremes from either side to ridicule? Something in me feels embarrassed when someone goes off either on religion or on science, because any human's possession of religious or scientific ideas is deeply felt. Best to tread lightly here. We don't have to make nice, don't have to join hands and sing "Kumbaya." But can't we live with what repels us, so long as the repellent thing does no harm? Yes, religious “terrorists” have done great harm. But is it the religion that animates the terrorist, or the terrorist spirit, packing a religious rationalization, that’s at fault? All of us gather in colonies, under different flags, and then comfort each other by sharing our dreams in a shared tongue. If those of another tribe approach us to share their dream, and we’re not interested, might we not simply and kindly turn them away?

War seems to be the alternative. And war, on the battlefield, in church or at the dinner table, seems to scale up quickly, given that we’re wired for violence. Everything we see is routed first to an evolutionarily ancient part of the brain, where the animal in us decides, in the moment, whether to fight or to flee. The machinery of anger and panic is always at the ready. That’s why I plead here for tolerance of what gives offense – not respect, not liking, just tolerance: of pointy-headed intellectuals, of illiterate Creationists, of the brother-in-law who jabbers endlessly or the acquaintance who quotes Rush Limbaugh.

After all, we are stardust.

We are atoms.

We are mostly empty space.

16.

Spirit Medicine

There is no shortage of exciting and promising avenues for studies of the efficacy of religion. In fact, there is, perhaps, only one thing to avoid: simple conclusions.

Kenneth Pargament
Bowling Green State University

It's time we stopped treating the placebo effect as a nuisance – something that rational humans shouldn't have.

Olivia Judson
Research fellow in biology
Imperial College London
New York Times/May 10, 2010

The fitness mantras are familiar. Exercise till you drip three to seven days a week. Eat your broccoli, squash, spinach, garlic, strawberries – all the brightly colored antioxidant-rich foods you can. Drink: moderately. Smoke: not at all. Down with LDL (the "bad" cholesterol), up with HDL (the good).

And maybe pray or meditate. Or attend religious services.

A Dartmouth study showed that patients with religious faith and social support were 12 times more likely to survive open-heart surgery. In a Duke University study of 1,718 North Carolinians, blood levels of an undesirable immune system protein, interleukin-6, were lower in people over age 65 who attended religious services at least once a week. A large survey of research studies about the connection between spirituality and physical health appeared in *American Psychologist* in January 2003. The authors went to lengths to separate the sound studies from the flawed, and they found no support for the idea that spirituality can slow the spread of cancer or speed recovery from acute illness, or that depth of religiosity makes a difference to health. But they found some physical advantage to churchgoing. The study identified 11 long-term investigations of the relationship between service attendance and mortality. After all the other variables that might affect length of life were factored out – race, gender, lifestyle, social support and depression, for example – attendance at religious services was linked to longevity. The mortality rate of churchgoers is 25 percent lower than that of non-attenders. The scientists also found that church attendance protects against heart disease – probably, they wrote, by encouraging healthier lifestyles.

Say amen somebody.

When some people hear this, they conclude there's a mind-body-spirit connection and that God's on the side of the devout. Others believe the studies demonstrate nothing more than the awesome power of suggestion and human gullibility. The placebo effect is powerful, they say. It can change the pulse rate and blood pressure, sexual response and gut function. It can even grow hair, if a study in the late 1990s was right: In the study, 86 percent of men taking a baldness remedy showed increased hair on their heads – but so did 42 percent of the men taking a placebo. But hold on a second, some scientists object: You've got to have a third group that receives no treatment and check to see what proportion of that group sprouts hair. Scientists who object to studies of religion and health may also find fault with studies of placebos and health: Both are just too woo-woo for some.

Myself, I think that if God exists, he may or may not heal those who ask, no matter how feverishly. It's that mysterious ways thing again. Consider Jesus. He didn't heal the moneychangers of their addiction to currency trading. He stayed away from the major population centers, choosing to toil in backwater towns. When he healed someone, he often said words to the effect of *Now keep this under your hat, OK?* as if he knew the perils of humans focusing too much on this particular aspect of divinity. Even if the benefits of prayer and meditation in some lives can be documented, the question of how these practices work remains unsolved.

•

Tim Daaleman is a Yale-educated former Wall Streeter. Today, he is a University of North Carolina professor and vice chair of family medicine who researches the connections between healthcare and spirituality. He's also a faculty scholar at the Duke Center for Spirituality, Theology and Health. Another prominent academy scientist searching for less conventional approaches to health maintenance is Duke's Harold Koenig. In 2002, Koenig wrote, in an issue of the *Journal of the American Medical Association*, that a "review of research published during the 20th century identified 724 quantitative studies, of which 478 (55 percent) found a statistically significant relationship between religious involvement and better mental health, greater social support, or less substance abuse."

Researchers with these interests will say that a lot of work needs to be done, that the cause-and-effect relationship between specific spiritual practices and health outcomes is unclear. And since the early 2000s, new studies have shown that religion can have negative effects. One study, for example, showed that switching churches may be bad for your health, especially if you're a Mormon or a Jehovah's Witness. Researchers noted that those who move onto a more relaxed church may start to drink and smoke; they also lose support from a group that provided them identity and may become isolated.

Columbia University psychologist Richard P. Sloan is a public skeptic of studies on spiritual practice and health. In the *Annals of Behavioral Medicine* Sloan reported in 2002 that research into the benefits of religion on heart health did not hold up to scrutiny. In a *New York Times* article reporting this finding, Sloan attacked those who conduct academic studies on religion and health for failing in some cases to analyze data with statistical rigor. After Rep. Gabrielle Giffords was shot in 2011, Sloan wrote in an opinion piece for the Times that a "fighting spirit" ascribed to Giffords by her husband wouldn't save her life. He wrote, "If people are insufficiently upbeat after a cancer diagnosis or inadequately 'spiritual' after a diagnosis of AIDS, are we to assume they have willfully placed their health at risk?"

It is objections like Sloan's that underscore the importance of studies of studies of the sort reported in *American Psychologist* and *JAMA*.

•

One of the most controversial areas in research involving religion and health is that of intercessory prayer, Daaleman says. That's where we keep a kind thought for Aunt Harriet, fighting a brain tumor in Biloxi, and ask our friends to do likewise, hoping she'll get well.

Keith Stewart Thomson, a former president of the Academy of Natural Sciences, writes of prayer studies, "Matters of the human spirit are not well suited to investigation by the scientific method. Whether prayer is a subject amenable to any kind of scientific analysis is a tricky question."

Intercessory prayer research is particularly difficult. For one thing, you'd have to recruit suffering souls who were extremely isolated; otherwise, the research could be contaminated by unwanted prayers from other people besides those in the study – or by cynics who, upon hearing of the study, would try to bollix the results. One National Institutes of Health study focused on intercessory prayer aimed at helping alcoholics. "When word got out about the study," Daaleman said, "there were people praying it would fail. How do you control for that?"

In general, Daaleman doesn't promote the idea that spirituality alone is good for your health. That can be dangerous, he says. Someone with appendicitis might rely on prayer and diet when she actually needs to go under the knife. Besides, Daaleman says, there's the obvious fact that people of faith, just like agnostics and atheists, die horrible deaths. The rain falls on the just and the unjust alike.

Nevertheless, Daaleman says, medicine simply can't touch some problems. That raises the issue of how to provide a sense of meaning to people with terminal illness. If spiritual tools help, it seems worthwhile researching them, so long as it is possible to design the experiment carefully.

Koenig wrote in *JAMA*, "Many patients have little control over their health conditions, which creates anxiety and, in some cases, furious attempts to regain control. . . . Religious beliefs and practices provide an indirect form of control that helps to interrupt this vicious cycle. They enable a patient to turn a health situation over to God and stop worrying and obsessing about it. Prayer gives patients something to do so they don't feel so helpless."

•

Scientists who aim to research the spiritual side of life don't win popularity contests. Their peers may suspect them of having a religious agenda. Those on the skeptical left get aggravated if the researchers get government support to do research or suspicious if the money comes from an organization like the Templeton Foundation, which has the goal of reconciling science and religion. Those on the religious right, on the other hand, are often deeply suspicious of science. But scientists who engage these questions aren't in the popularity business. The professional duty of scientists is, after all, to disturb the universe. There's a price to pay for doing that, as Galileo found in 1633 when, at age 69, he was put under house arrest for nine years.

That religion and science at times quarrel so vehemently is ironic. People in both camps have suffered for defying convention. Jesus, like Galileo, riled the authorities. Still, it's understandable: Scientists are protective of their culture and its rules, which are radically different from those that surround religious behavior. The perceptions of science rest on empirical observation, scientists point out; the findings of science are experimental, verifiable and replicable; spiritual beliefs aren't at all in that league.

Even so, I hope that scientists will keep trying to design good experiments to ferret out whatever can be discovered about the links of health, well-being and spiritual practice. There's something fitting about the scientist, who is devoted to the reasoned exploration of the unknown, examining the notions and practices of the religious woman or man, who is devoted to an intuitive approach. And vice-versa.

As science deepens our understanding of the benefits and problems of faith, believers may find themselves objecting to what they regard as reductionist explanations. Perhaps this ineffable thing called soul is just a ghost in the machine, prayer and religiosity nothing but wonderful placebos. Whatever is discovered, these establishments – science, medicine and religion – seem destined to cross and recross paths. They share a passion for translating the visible world, sourcing its doings to fundamental causes and leveraging what happens there.

They even share a history. In an editorial for the *Mayo Clinic Proceedings*, Koenig wrote that "religious groups built the first hospitals in Western civilization during the fourth century. . . The profession of nursing emerged directly from religious orders. . . ."

Neither religion nor science is likely to disappear soon, so why shouldn't they act decently toward each other? Some matters will be well-nigh impossible to study and others forever inexplicable. But religious people would do well – or will be forced? – to integrate scientific discoveries and the scientific world view within a framework of faith (and I'm not talking about "intelligent design" when I say this). Trying to grasp how scientists approach reality might give people of faith the willies, but refusing to buy anything that comes out of a scientist's mouth won't do.

The nuances of religious and spiritual belief and the diversity of practices is part of what makes its investigation worthwhile and exciting. There are many religions, not one. Ninety percent of the members of some churches believe in the devil; in other churches, the figure's more like 10 percent. Surely such a diversity of belief has consequences for the psyche and the body. A majority of mainline church members believe that God heals through doctors – but only a small minority of Christian scientists. The variables for study are plentiful.

In 1950, psychologist Gordon Allport wrote in *The Individual and His Religion*, that religion is a "white light in personality which, though luminous and simple, is in reality multicolored in composition." The multiple hues of any given individual's "religion" could have consequences for that person's health. Science should look at the rainbow and religion should welcome that.

17.

The Measurer of All Things

The Greek philosopher Protagoras said that man is the measure of all things. It's a grandiose niche, one that grows more difficult to occupy as we increasingly fail to agree on what a (hu)man is. The 20th century enriched our definition considerably; the result was both exciting and bewildering. At the start, we had Freud dividing psyche into three parts: ego, id and superego. By the end humans had been reduced to a spiraling molecule called DNA and its four chemical building blocks – adenine, cytosine, guanine and thymine. As a result of sequencing the DNA of various animal species and comparing the sequences, we know that if humans are the measure of all things, then chimpanzees are an extremely close second.

The Protagorean pronouncement reminds me of my long-dead grandfather, the Rev. Albert Katterjohn. He regarded himself not as the measure, but as the measurer, of all things. When Grandpa K. toured Europe in 1910, he noted in his diary that the portico of the Pantheon is 110 feet long and 44 deep; that 16 columns, each 46.5 feet high and 5 feet in diameter, support the portico roof. He also noted that the organ at Notre Dame cathedral has 6,000 pipes, 110 registers and five keyboards. The diameter of the hole in the Pantheon is 28 feet; the bridges connecting the islands of Venice number 368. Everywhere he went in Europe, he kept track of numbers.

This trait, along with his Teutonic severity and mechanical aptitude, makes me doubt our blood tie. While I have some of the severity, I lack his numeracy and the practical skills that made him, for example, capable of running a small printshop as a sideline to his ministry. If Albert had visited the great desert canyons of the Southwest, he would no doubt have tried to find out their dimensions and enumerate their geological features. Personally, I'm more interested in the contradictory feelings they give me about my importance on Earth. Staring into these canyons, I simultaneously experience both my meaninglessness and significance, which is perfect for a 21st century human who is typically, and deeply, confused about who s/he is or what s/he means.

On the matter of meaninglessness: When I stare into those canyons and backward into cavernous time, the brevity of my life stares back at me. I wonder about the river that runs along the bottom of Canyon de Chelly, *How did that bright string of water carve so deeply?* My mind answers, *Only after stretches of time that render my existence as insignificant as a speck of snow on a TV screen at the end of the broadcasting day in Oakley, Kansas, on, say, September 18, 1958.* As these thoughts sink in and I'm racing toward the end zone to put six points on the board for the forces of nihilism, a swift-footed thought catches me from behind: *It's only because of human beings that this "view" is a view at all.* Without human eyes and minds to perceive and take pleasure from a canyon, it's nothing more than a particle zoo out there – that's how subatomic physicists put it, anyway. Thinking that, I feel a flex of pride about my species. We may not ***be*** the measure of all things – but we do, in some sense, ***take*** the measure of all things.

But the complexities don't end there. All the sights I see and all the thoughts I gin up about them are only an imaginative construction, the creation of nerve cells, brain chemicals and electricity. We don't just know anymore; we know *how* we know, in increasingly fine-grained detail.

Take a bow, Old Measure-Taker, for trying to label and measure a world characterized by wobbliness and indeterminacy both inside and out.

The irony is that though we are the universe's primo meaning-making animal (or this solar system's anyway), the species is so good at it that we're having an identity crisis. One moment, we see ourselves on the mountaintop, the next in the toilet bowl, and both views are justified. From the cell's-eye-view of things, a human is an astonishing universe of trillions of usually cooperative cells, tissues and organs; from Earth's perspective, a human is one of 7.37 billion Homo sapiens (as of September 23, 2015), one species out of one-point-something million species; and in the eyes of the Milky Way, the Earth is only one of 8.8 billion earth-sized planets. With all this in mind, it's easy for a standard-issue earthling to become – as they like to say in Alcoholics Anonymous – an egomaniac with an inferiority complex.

Maintaining perspective is difficult. It's most difficult of all in relation to things at entirely different scales from ourselves. The most unknowable things are the smallest (massless gluons, which hold quarks together in protons and neutrons) and the largest (God? the multiverse?). Jack Miles, in *God: A Biography*, espouses an astonishing view: "God makes a world because he wants mankind, and he wants mankind because he wants an image." Miles writes that as Genesis opens, "[God] is portrayed, with apparent sincerity and unwavering consistency, as truly without a past and, though not without intentions, as truly without desires except the desire that mankind should be his self-image." Indeed, "God is dependent on human beings" for that self-image.

Sounds interesting – but are you convinced? I have trouble imagining humans as the mirror on God's vanity. And if we accept that, wouldn't God, these days, be having an identity crisis just as we human beings seem to be? (Are we the children of God? Of natural selection? Of both? Is

God leaning toward the Tea Party or the Green? Muslims or Christians? Does he have multiple personality disorder?)

I'm more in tune with a quote from astronomer Allen Dressler, made in a 1998 article in *The New Republic* titled "Science Sees the Light": "We've abandoned the old belief that humanity is at the physical center of the universe but must come back to believing we are at the center of meaning." That's a little less grandiose than thinking that God depends on us.

Still: "at the center of meaning"? I'd rather believe that we are both consequential AND trivial than to glamorize our role. We should keep in mind the run Australopithecus had. That species lasted from 6 million years ago to almost 1 million years ago, then vanished, for reasons not even we, the proud meaning-makers, know. If our species lasts another 10,000 years, we will have achieved 1 percent of the longevity of these hairy, dark-skinned, flat-faced, slow-footed, termite-eating midgets with a lifespan of less than 20 years.

Can we agree that with the increasing complexity involved in saying what it is to be human – given the ever-increasing number of terms and measures to choose from – it's also becoming harder for us to imagine what it is to be God?

Karen Armstrong would encourage us in that direction. In *The Case for God*, she writes, "Today, when science itself is becoming less determinate, it is perhaps time to return to a theology that asserts less and is more open to silence and unknowing." Instead, many people "feel that they know exactly what they mean by God," not realizing that it's only been since the end of the Middle Ages that that certainty has emerged. In the same spirit, they declare the Bible "inerrant," without knowing, as Armstrong points out, that the doctrine of the infallibility of scripture wasn't advanced until the 1870s.

Moving out of relationship to a God that we believe is like us into a relationship with a God who is unknowable is trying. Armstrong points to the fact that if we can't know God in the usual way, we "can neither feel nor have any sensation of unity with God." Ergo, being slain in the spirit is no longer an option. Nor is it easy to declare God responsible for the success of former quarterback Tim Tebow, as 43 percent of those participating in a web site poll once did.

For some, an indescribable Almighty is out of the question given the personal bond they feel with God. For me, such a God is frustrating but seems inescapable, lest, in reducing God to my stature, I lessen the divine mystery.

Puzzles

18.

The Stranger

I remember walking into a Dairy Queen, or some place like it, in Laramie, Wyoming. This was 1969, a year I hitch-hiked thousands of miles and generally looked pretty ragtag.

Anyway, there at the DQ, a young guy in a cowboy hat pinned me with a stare. That he was talking on a phone added to my sense of alarm. *Y'oughta see this hippy dipshit just walked in here*, I imagined him saying.

I picked up on that stare and imagined his rage because of an incident earlier that year. I was hitchhiking toward California when I got a lift about 3 in the morning from some kids.

This was also in Laramie. It was the last day of a celebration called Wild West Days. I offered cigarettes to the three guys in the front seat, complimented the Johnny Cash song playing on the radio. But at the end of the ride, the driver turned into a corral, stopped the car, popped open his door and said, "Let's get him."

The grace in that moment was that the two other kids stayed put, one even pleading with the driver, "Hey, let's go, he wasn't a bad guy."

"Get out," he said as he opened the door.

"But what did I do?" I asked. The plea failed. He kicked me in the leg with his pointy boots, but I didn't fight back. I just climbed out of the back seat, fell to the ground and curled up into a ball, absorbing more kicks. It shook me up, as did the indifference of a highway patrolman who stopped later and, after shrugging off the incident, counseled me to wait for dawn before thumbing again.

I say all this as a prelude to telling about a run-in I once had with an odd soul. Let's call him Herman. He scared me enough that I behaved in a way that shames me to admit, even though I don't regret it.

•

Herman was a visitor to town. I took him in after a fellow churchgoer, who'd enlisted in a Mennonite program designed to host travelers, phoned me. She had offered him room and board but then changed her plans. She'd be out of town during his stay. Could I put him up? I said yes. Herman was going to be staying at my house for five nights, the last three while I was at a family reunion in another state.

He had come to town from New York to attend a conference for pianists. After he was settled into the house, he told me he'd already been in the states for a while. He was unemployed, laid off by a tour-guide company for which he had worked. I asked why that had happened.

Because, he said, his co-workers envied him; he received higher gratuities from tourists. It didn't compute. *Why would a company lay someone off who was that good with customers?* I wondered, but didn't ask.

Herman's plan was to stay with me during the conference and then to spend another week at an abbey in northeast Kansas. He had inherited money after his father's death, and, unlike his sisters, he had decided, he said, to spend it. It was his way of honoring his father's memory. After leaving Kansas, he planned to go to Israel for six to eight months. He was trying to decide whether he should convert to Judaism.

In a guidebook that governs the Mennonite host program – I didn't know about the book until Herman referred to it – a suggestion appears that guests donate $8 a night to their hosts. After Herman had settled in, he talked about that guideline. He wouldn't be making a donation, he said.

That was OK with me, since I'd expected none in the first place. I was just trying to be a good host, in part atoning for my failure to do any other form of service to my fellow beings (a central Mennonite value). Hosting Herman was a way to salve my conscience.

I drove us downtown to a microbrewery for dinner, telling him along the way that I had a roommate named Steve who lived in the basement. By then, Herman knew about my plans to go to the family reunion, and he asked if Steve would be driving me to the airport. No, I said, he'd be at work. He said, "So you're not the kinds of roommates who exchange bodily fluids or give each other rides to the airport then?" The question seemed impolite given our brief acquaintance. A flag went up. I said we were only friends.

At dinner, Herman's tab was a little more than $11. He lodged a mild complaint with the waiter about the quality of the food. After we'd eaten, he asked whether he might write me a traveler's check for $20, for which, he pointed out, he would expect $8 in change. He was out of U.S. currency. *If I do this*, I thought, *I'll have to add to his tip or else stiff the waiter*. I wound up covering the tip.

This was not a good turn. I'm a penny pincher, one of those given to spasms of guilty generosity. My quarrel with myself about money is longstanding. My wounded inner Santa says I should be less miserly and give myself and others a break, while my Scrooge self wants to carry a calculator to reckon up separate checks at meals for five. Both parts have light and dark sides, but at bottom I'm a frugal person nagged and shamed by a jolly demon who's always slapping the frugal guy on the back and saying, *C'mon, guy, lighten up! Live a little! You can afford it!*

When you're deeply divided about an issue, you find that out in a hurry when you're around somebody who's taken a clear stand. The person who's resolved an issue that gives you fits is annoying.

As he and I were walking out of the restaurant, he sensed my discomfort. He said he really couldn't afford to tip generously. He had to watch his money. *You can spend six to eight months in Israel*, I thought, *but stiff waiters?* A judgment about him was taking root with surprising speed: *He's a taker, and I'm headed for a family reunion. What'll be missing from my house when I get back? What will he pawn?*

Back at the house, Herman told me that the futon in the living room, which I had suggested as a bed, wouldn't afford him the necessary privacy. Might it be moved into my study? This seemed reasonable. After all, he was going to be sleeping in the house five nights. Yet his meager tip and his using me as a currency exchange had raised my guard. It was late, and we compromised. That night he slept on a foam mattress and sleeping bag in the private room. To make more room for him there, we moved the ironing board into the living room. Steve, who'd met Herman earlier, had explained that he used the ironing board in the morning getting ready for work.

The next morning, when I walked into the living room, Steve was smiling broadly. He showed me a note that Herman had left on the ironing board. Steve thought the note a prank. It read:

> *Stephen:*
>
> *Did you know that it's be-kind-to-New Yorkers' week throughout the U.S. of A.?! With this in mind, might you be willing to perform the gracious gesture of including this white dress shirt of mine in your A.M. ironing-ritual for Wednesday? If you've the time, it'd be much appreciated. [be-kind-to-Kansans week is celebrated during the sixth week of March throughout the City . . .] thank you, Herman*

I shook my head, despair settling on me.

"It's no joke," I said.

Steve said, "I feel like ironing a few fucking wrinkles into the guy's shirt. Maybe burn a hole here and there." I understood. Herman had met Steve for five minutes and now expected – what?? – laundry service.

The next few hours I couldn't work for thinking about the days I would be gone from the house, and a feverish concern laid hold of me. How could I leave my house in the hands of someone who seemed to possess so little empathy or consideration? Nothing at all might happen while I was gone, but anything seemed possible. What would prevent him from running up a huge phone bill? I called the phone company to find out whether it would be possible to block its use for a few days.

Meanwhile, I launched a full-scale effort to analyze Herman. Part of me thought that he was only a garden-variety neurotic. I hauled out my Diagnostic and Statistical Manual of Mental Disorders, or DSM, a book used by therapists and psychiatrists to code the illnesses of their patients for insurance purposes. I diagnosed Herman as a borderline personality disorder (probably narcissistic) type. Herman's behavior toward me and the world also brought to mind an anthropological parallel, a former practice of the Asmat peoples of Indonesian New Guinea. The word *Asmat*, used by members of the tribe to describe themselves, means "the people" or "the human beings." Everyone else were the *Manowe* – or "edible ones." The Asmat were cannibals. Herman was sort of an Asmat tribe of one, traveling through a world of what he, perhaps, thought of as "the usable ones."

I had a hunch that Herman thought of me as one more human tool. We all use each other from time to time, of course, but usually do so with at least a trace of shame. I think I was offended as much by Herman's seeming lack of shame about using others as by any of his deeds.

•

That afternoon, a call came from a person who was helping to organize the piano conference. We knew someone in common, a woman who goes to my church, and the churchgoer had relayed my growing concerns about Herman to the conference organizer. She, too, had stories about Herman. He had left long and rambling phone messages on the answering machine of a local professor of piano participating in the conference. The professor had said he hoped Herman wouldn't show up. In the messages, Herman complained about the cost of lodging (which the organizers had gone to lengths to minimize), as well as registration for the conference: a princely sum of $50, which Herman had not paid in advance. Same day registration would cost $15 more. The person I spoke with said she would be watching for him and that she wouldn't let him crash the gate.

I needed help in thinking through what to do about Herman. I was confused, disturbed and determined to act – a toxic mix of feelings. So I met with Steve and Joe, a friend who'd been a helicopter door gunner in Vietnam. The son of a coach, Joe had played small-college football and was, with his bushy Fu Manchu mustache and bass voice, intimidating. We met at a bar in late afternoon. The first words out of Steve's mouth: "What do we know about this guy?"

"Well, we know that he's an experienced guest," I said, referring to his mention, at one point, of having found hospitality almost everywhere he went in the United States – including nearly all of the lower 48 states.

"And what does that tell you?" Steve asked.

"That he's probably been kicked out of a place or two or more and knows how to deal with attempts to do that," I said. Then a thought arose. I said, "So the only way to handle this is to give him no chance to argue about leaving." I hadn't until that moment considered evicting Herman.

The plan would take nerve to execute, a toughness that doesn't come naturally to me. I'd have to be nasty and rude and that would take an acting job.

Having hatched a plan, Joe, Steve and I stood outside my front door. I asked Joe to light a cigarette before we went in to evict Herman. I wanted a film noir edge to the encounter – Fu Manchu smoking a Camel would add the necessary touch of menace when we leaned on Herman. When I walked in, I went immediately to the phone and called the cab company. Then I went to Herman's room and knocked on the door. I told him that he would be leaving in a cab in 15 minutes and that he should pack.

I heard from inside the room a muffled "What?!" The door was still closed.

"You're leaving," I said. "Pack."

"Why?! What happened?"

"You're leaving. That's it."

I was sticking to the strategy of no explanations we'd agreed on in the bar.

The door of the room opened and he stepped out. I walked ahead of him into the living room and he paced behind. I sat down, bracing for his anger. I didn't look at him. I felt too guilty. But I was getting calmer by the second.

Herman stood in the arched passage between the dining and living rooms. "Is this the way you treat ALL your international guests?" he said.

"You're the first one," Joe chuckled.

"Did *he* talk you into this?" Herman asked, pointing to Joe. I said nothing.

"Well, I think I deserve an explanation," he said.

"I DON'T TRUST YOU," I said.

I hit every word as hard as I could, and then I did look at him, with the icy stare of a Wyoming cowboy gazing at a hippy. All this felt unreal, as if I were in a play.

"Well I think you owe me more of an explanation than THAT!"

"No," I said. "Pack."

I sensed that my reasons for evicting him would have sounded trivial, because my objection to him was, at that point, almost purely instinctive and visceral. How could I explain that something about him offended and scared me – without making myself vulnerable? I just wanted him gone, that's all, and I was willing to cut him cold to get that. It was actually a little thrilling to say NO to someone purely on instinct, without apology or argument.

And yet in retrospect, what I did disturbs me. Did I lure Steve and Joe to be my confederates in a lynching? Should I have paid to put Herman up at a motel at least for one night? Why couldn't I, so good with words, just talk to him or explain?

In a few minutes, the cab came, and Herman was gone. Some months later, I got a postcard from him.

R-M-,

The great thing about how you so dishonourably treated me there in Lawrence already a quarter of a year ago is how your own psychotic behaviour backfired on you vis a vis 'your' congregation – once word started to spread, people became ashamed of you and quite leary of your paranoia, and several approached me to apologize for your emotional illness and express their regret over how you abused the good name of 'Peace' church (Mennonite) & seek my pardon – Someone there @ K.-U. centre for research even lent me this snapshot of you taking a siesta . . . you never looked better! I hereby return your true likeness. . . .

The "snapshot" was a closeup shot of an assh . . . er, anus.

•

After I threw him out, Herman phoned a woman at the church and she and her boyfriend put him up. "He told us the whole story about what you'd done," she said. "He was, in fact, VERY strange. I remember walking into a room we let him stay in, and he'd put paper towels over all kinds of things. It was odd."

"But he seemed harmless to you?"

"Yeah."

I believed her. Herman never did me any harm. Yet remembering him, I still wonder about the relationship between what may have been his selfish (but seemingly harmless) grandiosity and its more pathological forms.

When is a person's deadness to the sensitivities of others or inability to calibrate or care about his effects on them no longer merely an annoyance but a threat?

Where is the tipping point between self-absorption and malice?

And if we believe we're in the presence of someone who isn't evil, but may be headed there, what's the right response – once we've offered him shelter?

19.

Aunt Stella

Why, O Absence, when the cry is most intense is the silence most stunning?

Martin E. Marty
A Cry of Absence

I wasn't there. But Aunt Stella, my godmother, was buried in a blue peignoir and a robe. Also at her request, the organist played Elvis Presley's "Are You Lonesome Tonight?" In the middle of the song, Aunt Lucille leaned over to whisper in my mother's ear, "Well, she ain't gonna be lonely tonight."

The joke was predictable – she'd be with The Man Upstairs, singing with the angels. The flowers I'd ordered contained a reference to this joke: I had written on my card, "To Aunt Stella, who will not be lonesome tonight." For me, the words were meant to commemorate a restless, giddy woman, my favorite aunt, who was, as my brother put it, about a half bubble off plumb.

Stella was my favorite because her delight in me was so transparent. While other aunts could be severe or distant, Aunt Stella seemed to take real pleasure in my off-the-wall energy, as if, when she was around it, she was able to sense something in herself that needed to get out. She laughed quickly at things I did and said. She let me iron handkerchiefs sometimes. She knew how hard I took defeat so that when we played games of rummy on Sunday nights with other family members, she sometimes orchestrated things so I could win a hand now and again.

•

Aunt Stella's death was welcome; she had gone into a hard-to-watch fade from 140 pounds to 80 by the time I made my last visit. There was no apparent cause. Suspicions of pancreatic cancer proved groundless. Pneumonia invaded, but her lungs were aspirated. None of a series of small strokes paralyzed her speech or her movements. She just stopped eating is all. Finally, they stuck a tube in her belly. But when the bleeding from the rectum started, they cut her back to dextrose and the next day she was dead.

My final visit with her lasted about three hours. She'd just been moved that day into the nursing home. At her former weight and at a height of about 5'7", she'd always been pleasantly round. She had big bones and, like everybody on both sides of my family, a big nose. My oldest memory of her was of a prominent and fascinating mole, a small and perfect bud of flesh at the juncture of the left side of her nose and face. Because it was so smooth, round and prominent and matched the color of her face perfectly, I couldn't, as a child, take my eyes off it. Her hair, as far back as I can remember, was an unchanging dome of tight, shiny silver curls.

But in the end she was just sticks and knobs, her hair dull, matted and disheveled from months of lying abed. Her roommate, June, smiled broadly and said daffy, senseless things. Stella herself seemed a bit daffy — too quick to startle and stare at anything passing in the hallway. It was as if she were seeing Fellini characters out there, and that may have been; her mother, Ella, had seen young girls stepping out of the bedroom mirror at the end of her life.

Dying in a way she never expected — not at home but shuttled among institutions — bred an intolerant rage in Stella. Or maybe it was just a shift in brain chemistry that produced fear that surfaced as anger. Stella would raise her eyebrows in disgust when June said crazy things. She would complain about the hospital where she'd been for weeks before her entry into the nursing home, how she had to ring and ring and ring at night to rouse a nurse. As her flesh had melted away, her laughter had left her, and her softness and sweetness dissolved. All the self-mocking and deference that had made her so dear to me disappeared. She turned into her opposite.

With bitterness came Bartlebylike refusals. She wouldn't eat or leave the bed. That exasperated my mother who, then in her upper 70s, had made a mantra of "staying active." I asked Mother to support Aunt Stella's obvious choice for death. Wasn't she just rehearsing for the Ultimate Inactivity? Why bristle about a torpor that Stella would not herself fight? But for Mom, it was hard. She treated Stella's naysaying as if it were a crime against God.

I sensed that Aunt Stella was in an existential crisis, even a collapse of faith, and maybe Mom did too, and that's why she was so upset. Like many women of her generation, Stella had not lived in a way that indicated deep caring for herself. Perhaps, at the end, the truth of that forced itself on her.

•

I took a tape-recorder to the nursing home because reminiscing seemed to please Stella. Better to try to connect that way than nudge her to eat a dollop of vanilla pudding. But her gauntness, anger and pain spoke against any tape-recording. The day before Aunt Stella died, Aunt Lucille and Mother saw the pain crest. Standing by Stella's bed, they listened as she gasped, over and over, "Help! Help! Help!"

I spent most of my three hours with her just patting an arm, telling her I loved her. Rather than elicit new stories, I recounted a few she'd told me, verifying certain details, as if to assure her they would be preserved.

The room was mostly silent. Stella did take grateful note when a breeze stirred. We found momentary common ground in complaining about a jackhammer rattling nearby, the noise relieving us of the duty to talk. We asked the nurses when the work might be done. Nobody knew.

I'd interviewed Stella four years before. At that point she'd been living alone several years, her husband, George, dead. This man, whom she'd married so early – he had been her Sunday school teacher – was, all his life, willful, bull-headed, energetic, talkative. But then, five years before he died, a stroke had left him with a child's bad temper and an inability to say anything other than a frequent, emphatic "NO!" (His physical helplessness heightened an already capacious urge to control.)

Stella's caretaking for George was a crowning touch in a life she gave to others without thinking twice (or maybe even at all): For Stella, duty was not a choice, and she was proud of the results. She would say, *They thought George was only going to live six months, but he lived five years.* One effect of her having lived so totally for others was that when those others died, so did her vocation and, with it, her identity.

•

When I visited Aunt Stella to interview her after George's death but before her health failed, my mother had come along. Stella was living in a trailer court. The shades were drawn, darkening the trailer's interior. Stella left enough space to peek out and check on the other residents' comings and goings. The tidiness of her apartment seemed confining, claustrophobic, as if Stella didn't want anything new in her world. When Aunt Lucille, who lived in the trailer next door, found a beau after Uncle Elmer died of stomach cancer, Stella didn't approve.

Stella's small living room was carpeted in orange and brown shag. On the wall was a reproduction of Warner's Sallman's *Head of Christ*, a 1940 portrait of a swarthy, handsome Jesus. A two-shelf bookcase was stocked exclusively with Reader's Digest condensed books. A large-print version of the *Upper Room*, a magazine of Christian devotionals, sat on a table. A 21-inch TV manufactured in an era when TVs were supposed to be furniture bullied the room with its size, but Stella said she didn't watch it much. I had given her a silly looking stuffed frog, which she perched on the back of her couch. She joked, "I polished the eyes before you came." When I went back to the bathroom, I peeked into her bedroom and saw more stuffed animals on her bed.

At my mother's previous visit, Aunt Stella had seemed more at loose ends than usual. ("The doctor says I've got a case of the nerves," she'd say, explaining why she sometimes scratched her shins till they bled.) On our way over to Stella's trailer, I had bought her a notebook and some pens. Maybe she could write her life story as a way of grounding that nervous energy. But the spirit of refusal so evident at the end of her life had already begun to move in. When I asked, she refused. That matched my mother's descriptions of Aunt Stella's passivity — how Stella could not be cajoled into doing volunteer work or much of anything else.

In those days, every time I visited she would try to palm something off on me. This time, I carried away one of my bronzed baby shoes. She wanted me to take away the condensed books, too, but I was as uninterested in them as she was in writing what happened to her when she was 14.

She couldn't sit still during the visit. One leg kicked idly. One hand caressed the other arm absently. It was as if that hand were trying, in a world without her mother or husband, to comfort her. Her patter was the same as always. Her sentences sometimes stopped before all the words had been uttered – the listener was left in charge of completing the lines. Perhaps someone important to Aunt Stella had, at some time in life, made it apparent that he or she wasn't listening. Maybe Stella kept surrendering in mid-sentence because she'd been crushed by the inattention of that important listener. At the end, maybe she thought God had stopped listening, too.

•

I wonder whether those to whom she gave her life so instinctively deserved it. Her mother and husband both possessed a sense of entitlement that found a match in her willingness to become a cipher. I remember a recurring scene: My uncle's face breaking out in a broad grin, his eyes narrowing to slits, as he described something Aunt Stella had said that he thought daffy. Still smiling, he would belittle her, then look at me, as if the two of us were in on a joke. Young as I was, I felt embarrassed. I sensed the pain of the taunting and wondered whether it shamed Aunt Stella.

As a child, her mother commanded her to be home by 3:30 every day, a half hour after school let out. As a result, Stella had no girlfriends in grade school. The mother's call upon her daughter's dutifulness never stopped. During our 1991 visit, Stella said, "On my wedding day, Mama said, 'I went to visit my mother every day, after I married. I expect you to come visit me every day.' So after I married, I went to her house every day. When George and me went on vacation, I had to call her every night. We'd go to Denver and cross a time zone and then I'd get bawled out for calling so late.

"Your Aunt Lucille says, 'My goodness, but your mother dominated your life.' I never would have thought about that if Lucille hadn't started talking about it."

Stella did not simply idle and chat with her mother. During her visits, she would wash and iron her parents' clothes, cook for them, clean. "And then I'd have to come home at night and do my own housework. Sometimes I was washing clothes till 11."

Ultimately, George and Ella wound up competing for Stella's services.

"Lucille says, 'I don't understand how George put up with that.' Well, after Daddy died, Mama wanted to come to live with us. We had two bedrooms then. But George said, 'If you have her here, I'm walking out.' Her and George hated each other's guts."

Instead, Ella wound up living with my parents the last five years of her life.

•

It wasn't that Stella never had a capacity to dream. As a

teenager, she wanted to be a nurse and begged her mother to send her to Chicago to study nursing. But that wasn't part of Ella's game plan.

Stella would speak with deep affection for the family's youngest, Walter, whose death at 25 after a three-day illness elevated him to sainthood, making him more revered and loved than any of the surviving children. He was a year younger than Stella, and timid. "Walter, you could shove him and push him and he'd never fight back. So one day this boy was bullying him, and it got me mad. Pretty soon, we were rolling around in the garbage, in a dumpster. I was beatin' him up, and he went home crying, 'I'm gonna tell my sisters. They're gonna get you.'"

The dreams of becoming a nurse and the assertiveness that helped her stand up for timid Walter disappeared, though, as she moved into her life's work of surrendering, of killing off whatever teenage dreams she may have possessed.

•

At one point during our visit, she said, "I cried all last night. I don't know why. And I'm not one to cry. Not at funerals, even."

She opened the Bible and took out a yellowed newspaper clipping, a piece of doggerel, which she read. In each verse, the poet described someone with a disability — blindness, deafness and so on — and then paused to reflect. The reflection took the form of a refrain that barely changed from verse to verse. The first refrain read, "God forgive me when I whine/I have two legs and the world is mine." In the next refrain, the poet said, "I have two eyes and the world is mine," and so on. It was the old count-your-blessings default.

Talk turned to the Gospels. Stella said she liked Matthew, my mother that she liked John. The room quieted for a minute.

Stella said, "I don't know why I'm here."

I asked, "You mean why you, personally, are still alive?

Or why God created humans and then left them to ponder about the meaning of it all?"

She said, "All of that."

At one point, Stella said, "Lucille says I ask too many questions. My fifth grade teacher said, 'I never saw anybody ask as many questions as you.' But how are you going to learn if you don't ask questions?" I wonder why she never questioned her self-annihilating duty to husband and mother.

•

The trouble with questions is that the answers may elude you or, worse, not be what you want to hear. I imagine Aunt Stella living in her trailer alone at the end of life, doubt stealing in. If she did not know why she was still alive, it surely wasn't for want of asking God – and what did God's silence, then, mean? Was God not communicating in a way she understood? Or at all? "I am forgotten, like a dead man out of mind," a Psalmist once cried out. "I have come to be like something lost." Is that what Stella felt?

If she were alive and experiencing the same doubt as she did back then, I would ask her about her idea of God and how that fit with what was happening. I didn't know then about the ebb and flow of faith, about those times of "spiritual dryness" described by monks and others on spiritual journeys, times when God seems to go on holiday. The idea among Christians that God sometimes makes his presence felt through withdrawal may have provided some comfort to Aunt Stella.

Something in her story brings to mind the elder son in the biblical tale of the Prodigal Son, the one who stayed at home, helping to manage the farm, while his brother busied himself squandering his inheritance. When the Prodigal Son returns home to a jubilant welcome by his father, the elder son gets mad. For Stella, there were no runaway siblings; my father and uncle both lived in the same city as their mom and dad. But they weren't ordered to show up every day. So wouldn't this thought have crossed her mind: *I helped my mother and husband. Who's helping me?*

Where's mine? If it didn't, she would have been a saint, and her anger at life's end suggests she wasn't.

I wasn't wise as a young man, so I failed to ask important questions of family members, ones that might have produced the answers I'd like to have now that I'm grown. I did not ask Aunt Stella the whys of her downturn and doubt she could have diagnosed it anyway.

So I am left to ponder the facts: She stopped eating, stopped leaving her bed, even to shit, and died for no discernible medical cause.

And a question: Is she lonesome tonight?

Elements of Faith

20.

How I Pray

[Prayer] takes place in silence and silence is the response you get, and mostly while you are doing it, you feel like doing something else. . . . Silence, it turns out, is redemptive, is generous. Silence is perhaps what a relationship with the Divine is these days. You could do a lot worse.

Rick Moody
"Why I Pray"
Esquire

A best-seller in the year 2000, *The Prayer of Jabez*, quotes 1 Chronicles 4: 9-10, where Jabez cries out to God, "'Oh, that you would bless me indeed, and enlarge my territory, that Your hand would be with me, and that You would keep me from evil, that I may not cause pain!' So God granted him what he requested." The prayer bothers me. Once the word got out that some folks had enlarged their territory this way, wouldn't that start a land rush?

Yet for many Christians, prayer seems to involve making requests that produce results. In fact, that spirit animated my first prayer, this cheerless ditty: "Now I lay me down to sleep/I pray the Lord my soul to keep/If I should die before I wake/I pray the Lord my soul to take." I doubt my mother knew the verse came from *The New England Primer*, first published in the late 17th century, which also gave us the grim verse "Xerxes did die/And so must I."

Christians who doubt that the Almighty is a radical interventionist still may return, in times of struggle, to begging God for help. I did. For a spell during my agnostic years, my rage at the friend who had cut me off had me begging God for the revival of the relationship. Nevertheless, in time some inner scold took to berating me for trying to use God like Extra Strength Tylenol.

Indeed, I have tried a variety of routes to approaching the Almighty, but at some point, I came to agree with philosopher Soren Kierkegaard, who said: "A man prayed and first he thought that prayer was talking, but he became more and more quiet until in the end he realized that prayer was listening."

•

In my case, asking God for favors never produced a lot of results. As a young man, I was a fevered mess, never so much as during my freshman year at the university. I prayed desperately for Jesus or God or whomever to give me a sign that they weren't fictions. But they didn't seem to fancy my desperation and were still. I left the church for 32 years.

So when I reengaged with Christianity at age 50 – I chose the Mennonite church in a Kansas university town, and now, some two decades later, I'm sure I was right – I was ready for God's silence. I have learned to wait, without expectation, for a little something, a nudge or word perhaps. (During that period of my life when I was enraged at my friend, my pleas for peace led to my hearing a single word several times, at various intervals: *Wait.* Eventually I learned to pray for an end to my anger, not the return of my friend, and that helped.)

Yet I still find it hard telling what comes from the divine and what's just background noise. I'm like one of those astronomers who, in the search for extraterrestrial life, use radio telescopes to sift through electromagnetic radiation, hoping to receive a telegram from the stars.

•

The 19th century psychologist William James managed to juggle his yearning for faith and his doubt in a way that kept them in tension without creating despair.

"We have heard much talk of late against prayer, especially against prayers for better weather and for the recovery of sick people," James writes. Then, giving a nod to science, he adds: "In certain environments prayers may contribute to recovery. The case of the weather is different. . . . Everyone now knows that droughts and storms follow from physical antecedents, and that moral appeals cannot avert them."

Further, James writes, the influence of prayer may only be internal, such that "what is immediately changed is only the mind of the praying person." When I read those words, I want to tell him that that's no small gift.

At times, I wonder whether I'm praying to the right part of the triune God. Frankly, I look past Jesus, thinking of him as the role model for us to follow as we engage with our fellows and of God as the healer. I forget or ignore the moment when Jesus tells Thomas, "No one comes to the Father except through me." About the Holy Spirit's role, Romans 8:26 notes that at times "we do not know how to pray as we ought, but that very Spirit intercedes with sighs too deep for words." Given my frequent bafflement about what I'm doing when I pray, I'll take all the help I can get.

•

At one point, my failures with prayer led me to a spiritual adviser, a bearded Episcopal gnome named Joe, who coached me in contemplative prayer, a practice that emphasizes prayer as a soul soother rather than a prybar.

Joe and I met once a week, working from Tilden Edwards' *Living in the Presence*. It contains 27 exercises in contemplative prayer. Before I describe a few forms of contemplative prayer, I want to define it. Thomas Merton, in the book *Contemplative Prayer*, describes it as expectant listening – "and yet in a certain sense, we [will] truly begin to hear God when we have ceased to listen." It annoys me when mystics say stuff like that, but then Merton tries to clarify himself, referring to "a higher kind of listening, which is not an attentiveness to some special wave length, a receptivity to a certain kind of message, but a general emptiness that waits to realize the fullness of the message of God . . . ."

Reading Edwards, I learned about centering prayer. You choose a word to signify your willingness to be quiet in God's presence, returning to the word whenever thoughts start to march through your head. I also experimented with *lectio divina*, letting myself enter and experience a scene described in a passage of scripture.

Normally, my mind is so crowded that, amid the racket, it's hard to hear God. During contemplative prayer, the street bazaar of consciousness shuts down, replaced by a warm quiet.

Yet after I return from this space, I keep thinking that there is more . . . well . . . more of God somewhere. I think that maybe all I've really found is a cool way to meditate, not the *mysterium tremendum*. Part of the problem is simply not knowing what to expect. God is said to communicate through dreams, fantasies, intuitions and the fabled still, small voice, but also, perhaps, through the chance utterances of friends or strangers, through accidental meetings, through losses and crises.

If I've seemed to narrow the motivations for prayer to petition and contemplation, I acknowledge many other motives, including, for example, confession, gratitude and adoration. Inside a cathedral in Peru, I once watched people gather around a statue of Christ. One man was at Christ's side, gazing, riveted, at his face, and reaching toward the figure. His rapture alone seemed a kind of prayer. I sensed he was in a relationship that I knew nothing about.

•

Church is for Sundays, a little more often if you're an evangelical. But prayer is a way to go to church every day – or every minute.

In J.D. Salinger's *Franny and Zooey*, Franny Glass becomes entranced with the idea that one might pray without ceasing. She hits upon the Jesus Prayer – *Lord Jesus Christ, son of God, have mercy on me, a sinner* – as a mantra. I read the book as a teenager and remember talking with my mother about the possibility of life's becoming a sustained prayer. The idea fit perfectly with my adolescent love of extremes, but I was more thrilled by the notion than the practice.

But the idea is still attractive. To pray without ceasing is to form a radical bond with God. Surely, such a bond would make things easier for those who struggle against doubt. That's what 17th century Englishman John Donne seems to be saying in a poem that begins, "Batter my heart, three-personed God. . . ." Donne wants his reason shattered, wants to be broken and made new, so that all doubt vanishes. He fails. "I . . . labor to admit You," he writes, "but oh! to no end . . . ."

Such a takeover would, no doubt, end the confusing work of knowing God. I'd settle for less than that. I'd be relieved just to be sure that what I have credited God with showing me or doing was, in fact, God's work.

21.

Soul Is the First Witness

. . . There is that mysterious thing cognitive scientists call self-awareness, the human ability to consider and appraise one's own thoughts. I suspect this self-awareness is what people used to call the soul.

Marilynne Robinson
When I Was a Child I Read Books

In its origins the soul was thought by theologians to resemble a miniature baby inserted by God into an infant's mouth at the moment of his or her birth. . . . At the moment of death, the soul-baby would then be expelled again through his or her mouth.

Alain de Botton
Religion for Atheists

You are a little soul carrying around a corpse.

Epictetus

Maybe it's because of the slipperiness of the subject that Thomas Moore wrote several books about the soul. Certainly, one choice to make in the face of a phantom is simply to keep writing. Melville did that about a whale in *Moby-Dick* and the soul is a whale of a topic. But it's not my choice to write volumes about the soul. For me, that would be like committing myself to a prolonged snipe hunt. I don't mind coming back empty-handed in the search for words to describe this thing called soul, but I don't want to give my life to it. So what I've got to say about soul is suitable not for a week's contemplation on the beach but for a car-pool commute.

An acknowledgment: I read Moore's books *Care of the Soul* in 1992 and *Soul Mates* in 1994, as soon as they were out; they have influenced deeply what you read here. At the time I was reading Moore, I had no idea I'd be trying to write about the soul. By the time I finished this essay, then went back to look at Moore and saw how deep my debt was to him, it was too late to do anything but offer this apology and begin. Now that I'm reading this essay once again, years later, I'm curious to know what I say in it, given that I remember almost nothing of what Moore said. I'll begin by introducing a few possible definitions of "soul."

Soul *n* **1.** *The whatness so strangely absent from a human being who has just died.* I stole this idea from a Catholic website, *New Advent*, where it is written, "Now the soul is the difference between a corpse and a living being." (Perhaps the writer had read Epictetus. But then such a definition no doubt comes 'round again and again because it's self-evident.) So try this. Take your ancestry, vocations, avocations, I.Q., hair color, temperament, character, DSM category, persona, appetites, hobbies, personal history and whatever else you think constitutes *You*; subtract your body; and voila! the soul.

Someone even calculated the soul's weight. In 1907, the *New York Times* credited Dr. Duncan MacDougall, of Haverhill, Massachusetts, for putting it at 21 grams. This was the difference between the just-before-death and after-death weight of his first study subject. (Five more dying people were measured and none of them lost the same amount. MacDougall was tickled pink to find that none of 15 dogs experienced a weight loss, proof to him that that mammal is, in fact, soulless.)

Soul *n* **2.** *The "something-more" of every living thing – Chihuahua, kohlrabi, oak tree or us – or a part of us that intuits that there is something more about life than meets the senses.* This is a positively stated version of definition No. 1 expanded to include, for the sake of the animists reading this, other living things. (They go still further, saying that rocks have souls, too, but that's enough about animists.) "Soul" might also be a name for our capacity to sense "something more" about life, the part that crooner Peggy Lee, of "Is That All There Is?" fame, missed out on.

Or perhaps "soul" is both inside and outside of us. In poetic terms, it maybe "the force that through the green fuse drives the flower," as poet Dylan Thomas put it. If you prefer the terms of cell biology, perhaps "soul" is the driving wheel for ribonucleic acid, causing it to copy a segment of DNA, hustle out of the cell nucleus and into the soup around it and start making protein. With apologies to animists, maybe soul is what makes organic life restless compared, say, to quartz. Plants make chlorophyll, animals make protein, but quartz does neither. That plants and animals make these things suggests that in some sense, organic life "wants" to continue, while quartz seems indifferent. Could the engine by which a self continues and, ultimately, the species of which it's a member endures, be called "soul"?

Soul *n* **3.** *A drop of the eternal – of God stuff – in all humans.* Perhaps soul is a little drop of God-in-us. Could God be like mercury, the soul a drop of godly mercury in each of us? My father once brought home a little of that liquid metal from the Coca-Cola plant where he worked. Kenny, his chemist friend, had given it to him to wow me and my brother, Bob. I was astonished by its properties, among these its mass and its ability, when rubbed on a dime, to restore its luster. But here's the amazing thing: Dropped, mercury splatters into "pieces," like little ball bearings, but these ball bearings, pushed together, absorb each other into a seamless whole. Maybe God is related to our soul in that way. Perhaps we get a dab of shiny God stuff at birth – stuff that's taken back into God when we die.

The conventional Christian understanding says soul does not exist before an individual life begins but persists after death, when there is reunion with God in Heaven or utter estrangement in Hell. But the idea of a post-mortem identity seems absurd to me. I side with Einstein, who wrote in his essay "The World as I See It": "An individual who should survive his physical death is . . . beyond my comprehension, nor do I wish it otherwise; such notions are for the fears or absurd egoism of feeble souls." It makes more sense to me that any soul I have would be resorbed into God (assuming that an "I" and "God" both exist) or just vanish (God's supply of mercury being infinite).

Soul *n* **4.** *The sum of the brain's nerve cell activity, plus a little something extra.* Yes, this sounds a bunch like definition two. I put it here because most scientists would omit the words "a little something extra." For example, Francis Crick, the co-discoverer, with James Watson, of DNA, writes in *The Astonishing Hypothesis: The Scientific Search for the Soul* that "The Astonishing Hypothesis is that 'You,' your joys and your sorrows, your memories and your ambitions, your sense of personal identity and free will, are in fact no more than the behavior of a vast assembly of nerve cells and their associated molecules." Crick writes that if mortals could build machines as complex as the brain they'd understand that our consciousness isn't a function of soul, but of brain mechanics.

Until we build those, however, I'm clinging to the notion of "soul" because it gives me a word to apply to moments of mystery and revelation. Most people have had meaning-drenched moments when their inner and outer worlds fused. For example, one day, while driving, I became aware in a way that was neither distinctly a thought nor a feeling that I was and am and forever shall be, world without end, *a singular event in this universe.* The context for this awareness was banal. I was nearing a stoplight when I knew, suddenly, that *no one would ever again be in this car at this corner at this moment having this awareness.* A thought followed: The envy I sometimes feel is useless, given that every human life is unprecedented and unrepeatable. The tingle I got having this (not so extraordinary) thought is what I have in mind when I talk about the "little something extra," beyond normal brain cell functioning, that may be a product of "soul." My stoplight moment, in which thoughts and feelings clustered into a sensation of Truth, seemed to me such a product.

Soul *n* **5**. *The something-about-us that we, and others, sense as our core identity.* Antonio Damasio, in *The Feeling of What Happens: Body and Emotion in the Making of Consciousness*, marvels that we can contain multiple selves, but an underlying unity. "We can be Hamlet for a week," he writes, "or Falstaff for an evening, but we tend to return to home base." Why? Damasio suggests we keep coming home because "a single organism requires that there be one single self if the job of maintaining life is to be accomplished successfully."

Now behind the assorted selves I deploy to meet the world, and beneath the interior disputes that sometimes rage between them, I, too, experience myself, for the most part, as one, not many: Could the word "soul" describe the distinctive flavor of that oneness – the vibe that others also experience when in my presence?

I'm feeling a spasm of guilt about my self-contradictoriness. I'm remembering what I said earlier, about the soul's perhaps being impersonal, the force that through the green fuse drives the flower or that makes RNA scurry around creating protein. Now here I am saying the opposite: that soul is the peculiar flavor of identity each of us possesses.

Soul *n* **6**. *That which sees paradoxes, even paradoxes about itself, and admits to complications in the face of our hunger for simplicity.* Is the "soul" the element that graces us with confusion and humility rather than steels us with certainty?

•

For me, the soul is as elusive as God. Is it when soul hides, or is ignored, that I fall prey to cravings, appetites, addictions – things material? The Christian sense of rivalry between the soul and the material world is implied in Christ's rhetorical question in Matthew: "For what will it profit a man if he gains the whole world and loses his soul?" As a teacher of introductory composition in the 1970s, I chose possible topics for my students to write about. One of my favorites was this: "Tell me, who are you **not**?" Few students took the bait. Well, I think it's interesting to ponder times and conditions that *don't* reflect my soul but instead expose my soullessness, times, for example, when my responses are automatic, when I am less present to all that is unfolding around me, when I'm less open to others. Perhaps it is my soul, lying somewhere below the drone of dailyness, that I'm searching for when I contemplate, meditate or pray. I hope that if I forge a deeper bond with my soul, the bond will amplify God's voice.

Not that volume makes things much easier. What I "hear" through the medium of the soul tends to be imprecise, suggestive and open-ended – hints and clues, in Whitman's words, not curt certainties. The soul doesn't speak in the firm language of thou shalts. It provides general guidance – love God, your neighbor, yourself – and lets you figure out the rest. The soul's work is to provide strategy, the mind's, tactics.

Soul sets a tone of softness, asking me to be more receptive than usual. At one point in my life, when I longed for a relationship or had begun one, I would pray for guidance. The answer I heard most frequently was simple: "Wait." God and soul together seem to have a program different from my preference for action. Patience seems a big part of the program. But different souls may have different programs.

•

"Soul" is a concept that even the secular society finds useful. In the 1960s "soul" became a mysterious something possessed by African Americans, something that certain honkies longed for. That kind of "soul" involved a courageous outspokenness wrought by deprivation and suffering, coupled with a willingness to slog on. The word connoted a capacity for deeper than ordinary feelings and sympathies. Soul fed the blues, which fused anger, sorrow, joy and triumphant self-assertion.

Some decades later, in *The Seat of the Soul*, writer Gary Zukav gave soul a New Age spin. It was "a positive, purposeful force at the core of your being. It is that part of you that understands the impersonal nature of the energy dynamics in which you are involved, that loves without restriction and accepts without judgment."

Maybe it's no accident that soul has been embraced so heartily by the popular, secular imagination at a time when personal identity is so strongly under attack. Maybe soul is the last refuge of identity. In the *Atlantic Monthly*, an article published in 2000 headlined "Soul of the New Economy" discussed, among other topics, Jeremy Rifkin's book *The Age of Access*. Writer Scott Stossel described Rifkin as spawning a notion of the "Thespian Persona," a personality for our time, one of fluid identity who can change depending on the demands of the moment.

Stossel: "'Autonomous consciousness is slowly becoming an anachronism,' Rifkin writes. 'In its stead is a new person who is more like a node immersed in a myriad of relationships.'"

Some nodes, of course, may like to think they have souls.

•

I look with nostalgia at the soul described by 19th century poet Emily Dickinson. There's something granitic and comforting about her sense of it.

She writes, "The soul selects her own society/Then shuts the door. . . . " It is unmoved by "the chariot's pausing at her low gate" or by the fact that "an emperor is kneeling upon her mat." Dickinson's soul is no ghost locked inside a vanishing identity. It is regal, full of authority, certitude, gravitas. If Dickinson is correct, we can ignore the soul for decades, as I did in my life, and it will still be right there, at our center, unmoved and unequivocal.

Our age assaults soul in a way that it didn't in Dickinson's. I wake one morning and, as thoughts drift by, I feel the sensations – the twitches, the tightenings, the rumbling and the easing – that attend each one; I keep watching, fascinated by the jumble of things going in what Buddhists call my "monkey mind." It also wears me out – *oh, no, another day in Roger's Multitasking World.* Then I notice that something in me is noticing this. Now I'm in a hall of mirrors. Suddenly I realize I'm hunting for my true self.

It is possible that "soul" is just the name of the first, and ultimate, witness, the part that notices I am noticing. If there is a God, and it is a Christian kind of God, the first witness is no blank slate. It has multiple perspectives, and can view the world through all of them at the same time. To steal a metaphor from gestalt psychology, it can look at a picture and see both vases and faces *at the same time.*

I will guess that when the first witness looks out from me at other people, it finds overwhelming evidence of our likeness – most people come into this world with a brain; two eyes, ears, legs and arms; 10 fingers; 75 trillion cells, give or take a few trillion. I also imagine it catching the flavor of other souls it contacts.

Because of this perspective, the soul feels the sorrow in our dazzling capacity to sniff out minute differences between ourselves and others and engender tensions about those differences. Don't blame war on the politicians alone. Each of us owns an exquisite capacity for drawing distinctions.

The soul knows that life within the house of the body could be less tumultuous. It longs for us to find ease. It would have us bring forward our best, evince humility and gentleness, forthrightness and integrity, calm and patience. It mourns the deformation of love as love twists into cruel words and deeds that betray our original tenderness and vulnerability. The soul is the angel in us waiting to meet the angel in another, so that these angels, like drops of mercury, can rejoin.

22.

The Reluctant Convert

I know I been converted/Do you?/Do you?

The Fairfield Four
"Standing in the Safety Zone"

Some don't go gently to God. The day C.S. Lewis went down on his knees in prayer he was "the most dejected and reluctant convert in all of England," he says in his memoir, *Surprised by Joy*. His conversion was a long march, beginning in adolescence, that took him through a series of "isms," including atheism, spiritism, idealism and theism.

According to David C. Downing's *The Most Reluctant Convert*, Lewis had "an almost mystical experience" at age 30 "while riding on a bus in Oxford." Lewis wrote that he had a wordless experience that day, in 1929, of "holding something at bay, or shutting something out." He felt he was being offered a choice to open a door or let it stay shut – with neither promise of reward nor threat of retaliation attached to his choice. Soon after that, he became the self-described reluctant and dejected convert he described in his memoir.

Christ became a regular in Lewis' life about two years later. He was in a motorcycle sidecar, his brother Warren driving. Downing quotes Lewis: "I know very well when, but hardly how, the final step was taken. I was driven to

Whipsnade one sunny morning. When we set out I did not believe that Jesus Christ is the Son of God, and when we reached the zoo I did." It wasn't an emotional recognition, according to Downing: "Rather, [Lewis] felt like he had awakened from a long sleep and now realized that he was indeed awake."

How did Lewis come to these revelations? After his pilgrimage through *-isms* and on the eve of the conversion, he had an important conversation with J.R.R. Tolkien and Hugo Dyson, Downing reports. The three talked deep into the night about metaphor and myth, Tolkien and Dyson arguing to Lewis that the myth of a dying God who sacrifices himself for humanity is worldwide, demonstrating a universal consciousness that redemption doesn't follow from virtuous works but as a gift from a higher realm. They "showed [Lewis] that mythology reveals its own kind of truth and that Christianity is true mythology."

"Having baptized his imagination with Christian myth years earlier and then having satisfied his intellect, it only remained for Lewis to surrender his will," writes Downing. "This was no small task, since he now felt he was not simply accepting a body of doctrines but submitting to a living Person. Christianity is, after all, not simply a philosophy, but a Way."

Lewis was famously willful. At age 4, he pointed to himself and said to his family, "He is Jacksie." Refusing to answer to other names after that, Clive Lewis thus became known as Jack to his family and friends. *My way*, Lewis declared in that moment. In the quest for conversion, "my way" is a high barrier to success.

My engagement with religion has improved my life. Prayer relieves suffering, quieting my feverish mind. Sunday mornings nested in a plastic chair at Peace calms my heart. Service – teaching youth Sunday school, for example, or washing dishes at the nutritional kitchen for homeless people – helps me bond with my fellow church members and the community. My faith studies have distilled the sometimes contradictory messages within Christianity to the knowledge that love means everything and that love's opposite, anger and judgment, are habits of mind I need to master, however slow my progress. I have followed an arc of *mind* toward God and morality. The deepest challenge to me in the matter of conversion is *feeling* it.

•

For many religious folk, a revelatory moment is crucial. In the year 386, a professor of rhetoric and Platonist named Augustine was at the end of his tether. Agitated and crying, he wondered, according to *The Confessions*, his spiritual autobiography, *How long, how long? Why not now? Why not is there this hour an end to my uncleanness?* Standing in a small garden, immersed in "bitter contrition," he hears a child's voice coming from a neighbor's house, repeating the words, "Take up and read, take up and read." So he opens a Bible to a passage urging seekers to forsake drunkenness, wantonness, strife and envy and surrender to Christ. "No further would I read," he writes, "nor needed I: for instantly at the end of this sentence, by a light as it were of serenity infused into my heart, all the darkness of doubt vanished away."

In *Personal Narrative*, 18th century American philosopher and Calvinist Jonathan Edwards was reached with similar force. Walking in the woods to contemplate and pray, he had a vision of the "wonderful, great, full, pure and sweet grace and love, and meek and gentle condescension" of Christ. Edwards was stunned thoughtless for an hour, "the greater part of the time in a flood of tears, and weeping aloud."

One part of me imagines such experiences to be given freely, as a result of grace. Another older and deeper part insists, however, that there can be no revelation without effort and striving. Then, one morning, somewhere between sleeping and waking, I saw this:

My hands work at unknotting a tangled ball of twine. As I work, two hands come from behind me, one on each side of my body, and join me in the effort.

A cushioning peace then entered my body for several minutes.

A week or so later, again in a hypnagogic state, I saw this:

My hands are working at unraveling the tangled ball of twine when once again two hands appear. But this time they lift my hands and place them over my heart, as if to say, Now rest.

These visions felt like an exceedingly gentle revelation. They made me think of something I read or heard once: that in a laboratory, if a sea sponge is pushed through a sieve so that its cells are separated from each other, they will gradually reassemble into a whole living sponge.

I wonder whether God is pushing me through a sieve that he uses to convert the reluctant. Will I realize some day that I've been reassembled so gradually that I didn't know it?

23.

The Jesus Confusion

There are many Jesuses.

To Jehovah's Witnesses, Jesus was the Archangel Michael before he came to Earth. Then he permitted himself to be transferred to the womb of Mary. After he died he went to Heaven and resumed his former identity.

In Mormon theology, Satan and Jesus are contenders in a contest where the winner gets a body to house his spirit. You know who wins that one.

The Jesus of the Assembly of Christian Soldiers, comprising more than a dozen churches in the South, sees Jesus conventionally, as a source of salvation from sin. But one of their teachings holds that non-white people don't have souls and so cannot be saved.

These, along with a variety of more mainstream views of Jesus, put God within reach of various imaginations, flesh him out, offer a blueprint for human goodness. Yet Jesus' conventional double nature – all human and all God, inseparably fused – makes him an unthinkable blur. Even if we accept the God/man as a possibility, though, Christians have been debating a long time about which aspect of Jesus – God or man – matters more. They've also disputed Jesus' reported utterances: whether he said them, which to stress and which to deemphasize.

And they differ about what Jesus' words and deeds mean in terms of politics: whether he'd hang out with conservatives or liberals if he were around today. In the *Proceedings of the National Academy of Science* in early 2012, researchers reported that these two groups divide in their perception of where Jesus would stand on certain issues, including such "fellowship issues" as leveling income inequality through taxation and treating illegal immigrants fairly and "moral issues" like abortion and gay marriage. The Stanford University researchers who authored this study of 1,236 individuals polled on Survey Monkey wrote that among survey respondents who claimed Christianity to be central to their personal identity, "liberals were much more likely to attach greater weight to teachings and tenets involving issues of fellowship, whereas conservatives were somewhat more likely to attach greater weight to teaching and tenets involving issues of morality." In fact, liberals surveyed claimed that Jesus would be more liberal than they were on the fellowship issues, while conservatives said Jesus would be more conservative on the moral issues.

It seems our guesses about who Jesus was may say more about us than him.

•

The orthodox view stresses His divinity – and yet, strangely, you won't find Jesus the Divine in Mark, Matthew or Luke, writes scholar Elaine Pagels, in *Beyond Belief*. In those three so-called synoptic gospels, honorifics like the "son of God" and "messiah" don't denote divinity; in the cultural context of the day, they could refer to humans, albeit ones with extraordinary gifts. It is only in John that Jesus claims a radical identity with God, Pagels writes, and "only in graduate school, when I investigated each gospel, so far as possible, in its historical context, did I see how radical is John's claim that Jesus is God manifest in human form." In her book, Pagels credits the trumping of the human Jesus by the divine one to the efforts of Bishop Irenaeus of Lyons, his admirer Bishop Athanasius of Alexandria and the Emperor Constantine of Rome. The vision of Jesus as a "man raised to a unique . . . status," in Pagels' words, lost out to an even more elevated Christ.

There was another loss as well: the idea that because humans are made in "the image of God," they, too, might contain a bit of the divine light that Jesus embodied. If that were the case, it would be possible for humans to strike out in search of God on their own. And if that were so, it's possible that no "church," in the collective sense, would have emerged or persisted. Pagels writes that the Gospel of John provided "a foundation for a unified church, which Thomas, with its emphasis on each person's search for God, did not." A religious hierarchy crystallized, the church holding the keys to the heavenly kingdom through its monopoly on baptism and other sacraments and, at rock bottom, its claim to be the arbiter of the truth in all its fullness. And so here is another split decision about Jesus: John posits him as a top-down savior while the Jesus of Matthew, Mark and Luke is more grass-roots.

In the book *Three Gospels*, Reynolds Price notes that John's "strangest departure" from the portrait of Jesus in the other gospels is that "John takes almost no notice of the man's ethical teaching."

He writes, "The parables of Mark, Matthew and Luke, with their implicit lessons on daily life and their guideposts to eternity; the eloquent moral teaching which Matthew and Luke record in such quantity . . . John has no room for a syllable of these." Price concedes that at the Last Supper, John does have Jesus commanding the disciples to "love each other as I have loved you," but Jesus was speaking to his "disciples only," Price says, asking, "Did he mean it for the world?"

Jesus the grassroots teacher is more popular than Jesus the Word with Christian liberals like those who constituted the Jesus Seminar. The seminar, founded in 1985, brought together scholars to sift through the gospels and discern what the historical Jesus actually said and did. Its founder, Robert Funk, published "The Coming Radical Reformation: Twenty-one Theses" in a magazine called the *Fourth R* in 1998. One thesis declared this: "We should give Jesus a demotion. It is no longer credible to think of Jesus as divine." It's noteworthy that the Jesus Seminar began its discernment by focusing on the utterances of Jesus, which they numbered at around 1,500, and not on the 400-some deeds. The gospel of Thomas – discovered in 1945 at Nag Hammadi, in Egypt – comprises nothing but statements attributed to Jesus.

Evangelical Christians don't much care for the Jesus Seminar. They are more interested in the Word made flesh than in the words and deeds of the Man from Galilee.

•

Arguments about Jesus range beyond the man-God question, of course. The basis for such arguments is, in part, the sheer abundance of conflicting information about Jesus – plus the fact that it didn't get written down until decades after his death. The oldest gospel, the Book of Mark, is said by antiquities scholar Richard Lattimore to have been composed after the death of Peter, around A.D. 64. John, the last canonical gospel drafted, was composed between 80 and 120. In short, the stories and words of Jesus were transmitted orally for some time and only then written down – in Greek, despite the fact that Aramaic was Jesus' native tongue. In addition, many other gospels besides the famous four and Thomas were written, some thought to be more spurious than others. Which, if any, portions of the other gospels might be trustworthy?

Why did the votes of Irenaeus and Athanasius count so heavily in constituting the early understanding of Jesus? In part because Constantine, the Roman emperor who finally made Christianity the state religion, said so. Should the spoils of controlling a story as crucial as that of Jesus go to so few? Do we dare reopen the story for discussion? Like it or not, cultural forces seem to be creating such a discussion right now.

Another problem with discerning what Jesus was really about is the biases of the four canonical gospels. Theologian Walter Brueggemann, writing in the magazine *Christian Century*, says that "the inherent word of God in the biblical text is refracted through many authors who were not disembodied voices of revealed truth but circumstance-situated men and women of faith (as are we all) who said what their circumstances permitted and required them to say of that which is truly inherent." Thomas Jefferson was less kind: ". . . The committing to writing of [Jesus'] life and doctrines fell on unlettered and ignorant men: who wrote too from memory, and not till long after the transactions had passed."

It's doubtful, for example, that Caiaphas and the Jews who persecuted Jesus were as bad as they're made out to be, writes Bruce Chilton in *Rabbi Jesus: An Intimate Biography*. It would have been in the interest of those early gospel writers to blame the Jews, Chilton writes, rather than rile the Romans, even if the Jews alone weren't responsible for Jesus' crucifixion: "The realities of power in Rome and Jerusalem, as well as Pilate's own temperament, made the theory of general Jewish guilt for the death of Jesus completely implausible in historical terms."

Do Christians risk quarreling – and a further loss of credibility – if they reopen the case of who Jesus really was? If we talk about the fact that the observer contributes unavoidably to what is observed? I don't think we can avoid the discussion. To the outrage of evangelicals, for example, the scholars who constitute the Jesus Seminar, in voting on statements attributed to Jesus, have deemed only 18 percent of them as authentic. Practically none of the sayings attributed to Jesus in the gospel of John was judged authentic.

Adam Gopnik, in a 2010 article in the *New Yorker* headlined "What Did Jesus Do?" summed it up well: "The intractable complexities of fact produce the inevitable ambiguities of faith. The more one knows, the less one knows."

•

As a child, I, like Pagels, was ignorant of the questions surrounding Jesus and the sacred texts about him, and learning about these questions today raises all sorts of feelings. How was I to know that some theologians and writers may have been using Jesus in the way a ventriloquist uses a puppet? I experienced only confusion: Who was this person who spoke from so many different centers of consciousness?

Consider the parable of the net in Matthew 13. That's the one in which the kingdom of heaven is likened to a net that catches both good and bad fish. You can guess what happens to the bad fish. The same will happen to bad folks, too "at the end of the age. The angels will come and separate the wicked from the righteous and throw them into the blazing furnace, where there will be weeping and gnashing of teeth," according to the New International translation of the Bible. In voting by Jesus Seminar scholars on the likelihood of a parable's having come from Jesus, it finished fourth from the bottom among all parables. Translator Stephen Mitchell, in *The Gospel According to Jesus*, writes, "It doesn't require much insight to recognize that we are confronting a very different consciousness here than in, say, the parable of the Prodigal Son. The teller of [the net] parable has no comprehension of the God who sends sun and rain to the unjust as well as to the just. He has split the universe into good and bad." How many people have had the Jesus scared out of them by writers anxious to put the fear of an angry God into them?

The good news is that with the gospels now disputed territory (though this presumption, too, is disputed), we have plenty to think and talk about. It feels as if Jesus is beginning to be raised from the grave of the old, old stories and sayings that have confined his meaning – and that this may open Christianity to some who haven't felt welcome until now. Mitchell's book, published in 1991, is subtitled *A New Translation and Guide to His Essential Teachings for Believers and Unbelievers*. I find reason for hope in Mitchell's including "unbelievers" in the title. *The Five Gospels*, resulting from the work of the Jesus seminar, has words attributed to Jesus printed in four colors – red, pink, gray and black. The colors reflect the scholars' decision, by vote, about the likelihood that Jesus actually said something (red), probably said it (pink), maybe said it (gray) and probably didn't say it (black).

A kind of millennial climax to all the talk occurred in the Dec. 6, 1999, issue of *Time* magazine. There, novelist Reynolds Price, mentioned earlier as the author of *Three Gospels*, "examines what faith and historical research tell us after 2,000 years and emerges with his own apocryphal gospel," according to the writer of a teaser introduction to the article, headlined "Jesus of Nazareth: Then and Now."

•

Even if we believe Matthew, Mark, Luke and John to be the truth, the narrative is still hard to follow. No matter how many times I read the gospels, they seem to turn into a slurry of miracles, wise sayings and allegorical fables. I find myself immersed in a disjointed but fabulous dream replete with loaves and fishes, doves descending from heaven and demons cast into pigs that then stampede down a hill and drown; a dream of wine and water and crowds; of tiny backwater Nazareth and big, self-important Jerusalem. Here I read about a demon-possessed man living in a cemetery; here about a leper; here a paralytic; here someone lowered through a roof for Jesus' healing touch. One woman can't stop bleeding, another is about to be stoned to death. Jesus saves them both. There's a mother Mary and a demon-possessed-whore Mary. How do the Romans and the Jewish bigwigs at the temple fit together? Who's Herod, and what's his relationship to Pilate? Besides the confusion at the surface, there's back-story bewilderment.

"I love to tell the story" were the words of a hymn we often sang at my church, but frankly, I didn't love to hear it told. Neither myth nor history, it hovered in some uneasy place between the two. The story's being served up a few verses at a time each week didn't do it justice either. It seemed confusing, confused. No wonder one of the followers of Valentinus (a leader of Gnostic Christians, a group that gave more free rein to the individual imagination when it came to the reading of scripture) sought to amalgamate the four canonical Gospels into one.

The density and confusion of the Gospels require that as grownups we set about taking possession of the story ourselves. Thinking people who approach Jesus will do well to read the primary texts to the bottom, then ponder what scholars have said, talk to their fellows and brace against frustration. I admit despair, yes, when I think about the crucial years that passed between the crucifixion and the written stories of the events leading up to it; the passage of 2,000-plus years, during which social and political forces of empire and the sheer grinding power of time caused some versions of the story to be disappeared and those that remained bent to serve various purposes; the translational leaps that had to be made between Aramaic, Greek, English.

It is an obligation to pry the metal of meaning from this ore and not surrender too easily, but it's hard not to feel defeated before I even begin. (I say this because I have never read the Bible through completely, I'm ashamed to admit, while my wife has done so four times now.)

It's not in me, or hasn't been to date, to be the kind of Christian who, when approached by someone who asks me, "Do you believe in the Lord Jesus Christ?" can answer with an affirmation that's like a gavel coming down in a courtroom. Instead, I stand there wondering, *Which one do you have in mind? The miracle-maker? The sage? The sarcastic Jesus? The teller of parables? Are you asking whether I believe in YOUR Jesus?*

Nevertheless, I feel obliged to pursue this mystery no matter how complex the labyrinth.

•

Yet, oddly enough, some take comfort in knowing that the story of Jesus has been subject to much tinkering and reinvention. Yale scholar Jaroslav Pelikan, writing in *Jesus through the Centuries: His Place in the History of Culture,* makes this clear:

"The later chapters of this book show that as respect for the organized church has declined, reverence for Jesus has grown. For the unity and variety of the portraits of 'Jesus through the centuries' has demonstrated that there is more in him than is dreamt of in the philosophy and Christology of the theologians."

Given this, is there not a place, short of heresy, for what Price calls "restrained imagination" as an "honest reaction to the Gospels' limited provisions"? After all, the product of such contemplation can be "a usefully expanded narrative," Price writes.

I don't want the old, old story to be placed beyond the reach of my "restrained" imagination, no matter how limited that imagination may be or how untrained or how historically uninformed. Reaching into the gospels with my heart, mind and soul may be the best way for me, or anybody, to reclaim the story of a remarkable life, a story whose interpretation the established church laid claim to centuries ago. One of the attractions of the Mennonite church for me is that it vests its members with the authority to act as readers of sacred text. The Bible "should be read and interpreted collectively by the whole congregation," writes Mennonite thinker John Roth in his book *Beliefs: Mennonite Faith and Practice*, referring to a "participatory process of interpretation."

I admit feeling a need to apologize for saying, in effect, *Begone, Gospel Experts! I'll figure this thing out on my own!* If, lying on my deathbed, I realize that I have been misreading the texts and missing the point, I guess I'll be sorry. On the other hand, if I'm still in my right mind, I may recall what Chief Broom, the schizophrenic Indian narrator of the novel *One Flew Over the Cuckoo's Nest,* says near the start of the novel: "It's the truth even if it didn't happen." That's a comforting thought.

24.

So Here's *My* Jesus

At a writer's workshop one summer, essayist Phillip Lopate wrote on a piece I'd submitted, "Am not sure yet what role Jesus Christ has in the God search." After class I pleaded with Lopate: "Please don't ask me about Jesus. God is hard enough to deal with." By "deal with" God I meant understand, explain, excuse, detect, imagine, let Her be Herself (or It, Itself), trust, obey, feel much about, propitiate or ponder. But I admire Lopate's essay writing and have ever since, on a first date, a woman shared with me his essay collection *Against Joie de Vivre*. I eventually married that woman, and though we divorced, Lopate was a legacy of our love, and his uncertainty about what I made of Jesus forced me to grapple with the question of God's son.

I put the question off as long as I could, but no matter: It kept staring at me, like a cat before mealtime. My first effort turned into the essay that precedes this one, with its focus on Jesus' unknowability given the passage of time between his death and the first accounts of his words and deeds; the multiple gospel accounts shading his meaning this way or that; the problems imposed by translation; the overlays of editorial bias and political agenda; the gloss of legend; and our inevitable failure to grasp fully or partly – or even barely – the historical, geographical and ideological context in which Jesus lived. The former chair of religious studies at the University of Kansas, Paul Mirecki, told me this: “I think a historically objective picture of Jesus is not retrievable. Religion is an art form not a historical science. It's closer to Monet than Einstein, impressionism than realism.”

Another reason to avoid the Jesus question: Others have spent so much longer thinking the man/God through. And they've studied Greek or Aramaic to get closer to the source materials. They've done the heavy lifting, leaving the dilettante niche to folks like me.

Then there's the problem of the residue of Jesus memories from my childhood. There was this song “Tell Me the Stories of Jesus,” a sappy number but easy for us kids to sing. Yet what, I wonder all these years later, is a wayside? I recited words aloud each Sunday that indicated he was born of a virgin and rose from the dead. (Footnote: the Apostle's Creed, where that language appears, takes a flying leap from the virgin birth to Pontius Pilate, sailing right over the life, works and words of Jesus. I appreciate the Mennonite church both for attending to the years between Jesus' birth and arrest and for maintaining a certain skepticism about creeds in general.) What did the word “virgin” mean to me, a Midwestern 8-year-old in 1954? Nothing. Is it a mistake to encourage children to mouth words and profess beliefs they can't possibly understand?

•

But I digress. As to the role of Jesus in the God search: Jesus embodies God's power through the miracles attributed to him. Now although I don't reject these, I don't care much for them. They seem to me to fuel an impulse to use prayer to leverage God into bestowing miracles on behalf of oneself and those near and dear – or if not miracles, then protection, as in the “traveling mercies” often requested at Peace Mennonite for those beloved who are out on the road somewhere. It's natural to want ease and safety for our pals, of course, and church is a community in which we can practice caring for those who aren't our closest friends. But wouldn't it be well to enlarge the circumference of our circle of caring to include utter strangers? At its best, religion does do that (see the Good Samaritan story) but even at Peace Mennonite, service tends not to extend very far into the public realm. I think that makes us a pretty poor example of Mennonitism, but then I've been in few other Mennonite churches.

Back to the miracles of Jesus. They and the bodily resurrection of Christ are central to fundamentalists. A 2009 Harris poll showed that 76 percent of Catholics, Protestants and Jews believe in miracles. Just 63 percent of the Jews polled professed belief, compared with 95 percent of born-again Christians. I would guess that a good many members of our church would stare at the floor if they were queried about their belief in the more astonishing feats of Jesus, but I'm not really sure: Absent an adult Sunday school, few occasions arise to talk about this or that feat. And these feats generally seem to interest Mennonites less than Jesus' ethics.

On the other hand, the long-term drift of churches away from Jesus as the miracle man isn't altogether comforting. Jesus as supersage . . . as contrarian counselor who movingly insists (in Matthew and Luke though not in Mark and John) we love our enemies . . . doesn't quiiiite get me where I want to go. Lao-tzu or Buddha also have wisdom. Some part of me still yearns for signs and wonders, for a Jesus who is as present as my shadow. I want the possibility of a watchful and caring spirit guardian – as the Rolling Stones sang, *We all need someone we can lean on* – and so I pray ***as if*** that Jesus exists, though less as time passes and my faith matures.

Sure, I sometimes get a wistful yearning for an ecstatic experience of the presence of the divine that seems to be easy for those who are more likely to believe in the devil than in evolution. But I'll probably have to settle for a role model rather than a buddy.

•

What most fascinates me about the role model Jesus is his unpredictability, his complications. There's so much more complexity than I undertood when I was young. You might expect God's son to be rule-bound, for example. If the father engineers a universe that depends, for the emergence of life, on very precise conditions being met, might not the son also likely be a stickler for the rules? In fact, though, Jesus sometimes broke rules. When his disciples hiked through a field picking corn on a Sabbath or when he performed a healing on that day of rest, the Pharisees challenged him. In response, Jesus took a stand that said, in effect, *Human need trumps rules.* When he told the folks who crowded around him that they must be prepared to leave their families to be his disciples, he's in effect saying that honoring one's earthly parents – the stuff of the Fifth Commandment – isn't always, in practice, straightforward.

Nevertheless, principles are what make Jesus famous. An aristocrat asks him how to inherit eternal life, so Jesus ticks off a few of the commandments, then adds something about selling everything he has, giving it to the poor and following him. A lawyer who's trying to trip him up is told that the two greatest commandments are to love God with everything you've got and your neighbor as much as yourself.

Now Jesus didn't just test the nerves of temple legalists. He also frustrated the disciples. When a woman buys an expensive ointment and pours it on his head, some of his followers protest. *Jesus, we really could have used that money for other projects.* He'll hear none of it. He praises what she has done as "one of the good works" and then adds, "She has done what was in her power to do. . . ."

Jesus is an equal opportunity savior. He pals with people without regard to nationality, class, occupation, gender, physical condition or disability. He even loves Romans – he singles out for praise the faith of a centurion whose servant he then heals.

Jesus apparently loves to eat and drink – "a glutton and a drunkard, a friend of tax collectors and sinners" is the way Jesus imagines many see him, he says in the seventh chapter of Luke. At one point in his ministry, speculates

Bruce Chilton in *Rabbi Jesus*, Jesus might even have had a paunch: "Capernaum brought him times of plenty, and – as his message became more and more popular – little requirement for manual work . . . Shorter than the norm, overweight, and tending to baldness, nothing about Jesus in physical terms . . . can explain his magnetism."

Dead certain about some things, Jesus, at other moments, is surprisingly flexible, humble enough to change his mind when challenged. A Canaanite woman wants Jesus to exorcise a demon from her daughter. Jesus says, "Look, ma'am, I was sent to Earth to help these Jews – they're my children. I can't take care of everybody. If I did, it'd be like feeding my dogs instead of my children." She says, "But even the dogs eat the crumbs that fall from their master's table." With that, Jesus admits that she has "great faith" and heals her child.

Interestingly enough, Jesus seems to have some hang-ups about his family. Perhaps that's logical, Chilton says, given that Jesus certainly would have been labeled a bastard in his hometown. When someone notes that his mother and brothers are standing outside the rim of a crowd, waiting to see him, Jesus corrects the speaker, "My mother and my brothers are those who hear the word of God and put it into practice."

Amid these fluctuations, what are the constants in Jesus' character? He is preternaturally sensitive to those afflicted in health or spirit – a sick woman has only to touch the hem of his garment for him to experience a loss of power; respectful of those who give abundantly from the little they have; supportive of those who willingly shed the character armor of a former life and start a new one, of those who demonstrate a faith that leaps without knowing where it will land. He wants humans to risk connection, to each other and to a God they can't know through the senses. Charles W. Hedrick, distinguished professor of religion at Missouri State University and author of *When History and Faith Collide: Studying Jesus*, told me that Jesus is a "multi-sided human being who simply cannot be reduced to a one liner and do justice to all of the fragments." But when I pressed about the matter of Jesus' essence, he said, "If you push my back to the wall, I would say the one saying of Jesus that reflects Jesus at his finest would be 'love your enemies.'"

I used to be cynical about that statement. Today, as I meditate on it, it seems to me to be a koan: Most of us find it as hard to imagine loving an enemy – **REALLY** loving an enemy – as to hear the sound of one hand clapping. This is not a simple order to "live-and-let-live." It means reaching down into yourself when you're around someone who hates you, or vice-versa, and bringing up water to share rather than sand to throw in his face or salt to rub in his wound. It means doing something other than what comes naturally: fighting, fleeing, freezing. What the Buddhists call unconditional friendliness amounts to the same thing. That Buddha and Christ, had they met, would have shaken hands on this point makes it overwhelmingly important that we ponder it.

Correlated to Jesus' love is his ability to take a fall for something he never did and accept being known as someone he is not. In Luke 22:37, he says, ". . . I tell you these words of scripture have to be fulfilled in me: *He let himself be taken for a criminal.*" Yale scholar Jaroslav Pelikan, whom I mentioned in the previous chapter, writing in his *Jesus through the Centuries: His Place in the History of Culture*, cites the foreshadowing of a Christ-like man in just these terms in Plato's *Republic*. In part II of the *Republic*, Glaucon and Adeimantus, two young men, are talking to Socrates. Glaucon proposes that they imagine "two men, one just, the other unjust, given full license to do whatever they like, and then follow them to observe where each will be led by his desires."

Each is given a magic ring. It confers invisibility, so that they may do as they wish, seizing power and glory. No one expects either to have the strength of mind to be good under these circumstances. The two men are "perfect types," Glaucon says. The unjust man has "the full complement of injustice. We must allow him to have secured a spotless reputation for virtue while committing the blackest crimes." The just man, meanwhile, will have everything stripped away from him but his capacity for justice. He will be "denied every advantage [the unjust man] enjoyed. Doing no wrong, he must have the worst reputation for wrong-doing, to test whether his virtue is proof against all that comes of having a bad name; and under this lifelong imputation of wickedness, let him hold on his course of justice unwavering to the point of death."

What would be the fate of such a man? Glaucon says, "Our just man will be thrown into prison, scourged and racked, will have his eyes burnt out, and, after every kind of torment, be impaled."

In Jesus' calm acceptance of the betrayals of Judas and Peter; in his staying the hand of the disciple who cuts off the ear of the high priest's slave at the moment of Jesus' arrest; in his refusal to answer Pilate's questions directly or to taunt Pilate; and in his utter silence in an appearance before Herod, his perspective seems to have changed from just a few days before when, entering Jerusalem, he banged around the temple, turning over tables. He knows that on a planet rife with bullshit, his words and deeds **must** align. To answer Lopate's question then: the place of Jesus in my God search is to model for me the possibility of seemingly unattainable kindness and patience, which I need to reach toward even though they remain beyond my grasp.

•

When I stopped going to church as a teenager, Jesus was weighing on my mind. He could not have seemed more distant. He was the Jesus of the Gospel of John, possessed of a perfection that shamed me. In *Penseés*, Pascal writes that "Jesus Christ is a God whom we approach without pride, and before whom we humble ourselves without despair." As a prideful and despairing adolescent, I couldn't approach Jesus at all.

C.G. Jung says that to understand a dream, we need to turn it over and over in the mind so that all of its meanings can emerge. Christ was once a man who walked the Earth. But far more significantly, he was and is a cultural dream. As I turn that dream over in my mind today, it is far different for me than it was in childhood. I hope that I see Jesus with the kind of "restrained imagination" that novelist Reynolds Price said he used in mulling the son-of-God's story for a December 1999 issue of *Time* magazine. Adding to the meaning of sacred text through imaginative interpretation and amplification is a time-honored tradition. Jews even have a special word for it: Midrash.

As I perform my own Midrash on the gospels, one of Jesus' most striking features after his arrest seems to me to be that he did nothing but speak his truth those last days on Earth. He become a non-doer, a non-resister, at a point when anybody else would have been kicking and screaming, running and fighting, denying and betraying, blaming and bargaining. Is it because Jesus knew the script, the part he was destined to play, that he acted this way? To say that makes him less, I think. I believe he wound up on a low cross at Golgotha because at the end of his life he lost the instinct for flight or fight that, in emergencies, possesses merely human beings.

Jesus' behavior suggests how eerily powerful it is, in some circumstances, to do "nothing" in the conventional sense. Our brains are built so that every visual input into the central nervous system goes first to a primitive sector. Then, a fraction of a second later, the input goes to the cerebral cortex for more complex processing. Jesus had an extraordinary ability to process input at the cortical level rather than the primitive one. When everyone else took flinty positions, he turned to water. God the father, betrayed over and over again in the Old Testament, becomes violently upset. God the son, betrayed by the political and religious establishments, not to mention one of his own disciples, stands still and takes it and, in return, does the impossible: He loves. Most heroes are famous for their action. Very late in his life, Jesus' heroism involves not-doing. In the end, he appears not to care about whether the impression he is making is one of strength or weakness. The remarkable fact is that if Christ is God, then we must conclude that God, around 2,000 years ago, quit ranting and raving about humanity's flaws and betrayals and showed us, through his son, how to love people no matter what they do.

What is the role of Jesus in the God search? The answers are many, but I'd say Jesus shows us that at times God can do a full 180. If we are made in the image of God, we must, at times, strive to do the same.

Epilogue

25.

Take What You Want and Leave the Rest

. . . The downfall of many a faith has been its unreasonable insistence that adherents must eat everything on the plate.

Alain de Botton
Religion for Atheists

For 20 years, I had nothing to say about a God that was missing in action from my life. Then, during a spell of unshakable rage and gloom, I prayed. And prayed. And prayed some more.

As soon as I mended a bit, I stopped. I looked in the rearview mirror in disbelief. *Me? Praying? How could I sink so far?* After this flirtation with God, nearly a decade passed before I stepped into a church under my own volition. Because doing this was a public act, not private – as prayer is – it was embarrassing. *What will my friends think?*

I've gone to that church now for 18 years. In 2004, I married Barbara Yoder. Two years after that I became a member of the church. Why? This statement is what I read aloud the day I joined:

Saying why I want to become a member of Peace takes me back to my decision to ask Barbara to marry me. I asked her to marry me because I just **knew**. *I just knew, after a lot of confusion on my end, that we belonged together because of my love for her and her love for me. Today, I can stand here and say that I* **know**, *after much doubt and confusion on my part, that Peace Mennonite and I are an item. Barbara was important. By small, gentle nudges, she brought me around. That is, she has asked me from time to time why I have not joined the church. I'm not a joiner, and that is the truth. I joined no fraternity at the University of Missouri, and I've never joined a Kiwanis Club or become a Lion. In not being a joiner, I honor my father. But unlike my father, who was too wounded to participate fully in church or join anything else, I've taken the plunge. I've found myself more often buoyed than weighted by our collective life. I love the people here. I love the intimacy. I love this church, where I met Barbara, and now I want to marry it, too.*

I was polite enough not to mention the obvious: that marriage is sometimes a struggle. Nothing about religion or the church comes easily to me, a sentiment I sense is shared by some of my fellow congregants.

In my childhood, people got recognition each year for perfect attendance at church. Nobody at Peace Mennonite Church would qualify. We have been, since the volleyball game in the early 1970s that helped launch the church, a congregation of imperfect attenders who took our marbles and went home when the place upset us.

•

One of the most difficult issues in the past 30 years has been determining how or whether to welcome gays and lesbians into the church. As I wrote earlier, in 1983, the pastor of what was then called the Lawrence Mennonite Fellowship, John Linscheid, came out. Seventy-five percent of those in the fellowship opposed his continuing as pastor, but nothing had been settled when Linscheid quit in 1984. Conservatives left the fellowship, which was then renamed Peace Mennonite Church.

In 2001, the year we drafted a welcoming statement that echoed the language of the Supportive Congregations Network, a few conservatives defected. But within a couple of years, for various reasons, some of the liberals who'd "won" followed suit. Barbara likes to say (in reference to the departed) that some of those wanted us to be a Zennonite, not a Mennonite, church.

People still come and go. But things have settled down since our current pastor, a woman in her 30s named Joanna, took over in June 2006. In 2010 Joanna was asked by two women from Leavenworth, Kansas, whether she would perform a covenant ceremony for them. They'd failed to find a pastor in their hometown who'd do the job. Joanna called a meeting to determine the congregation's feelings about this. I feared another ugly rift so I skipped the meeting. After some discussion, the matter earned congregational consensus because everyone agreed that Joanna, in performing the service, would be acting from conscience.

Nonetheless, she got in trouble with the Western District Conference, which our church belongs to. The conference Leadership Commission let her retain her credentials, but the matter wasn't closed. A few Mennonite churches in Kansas and Oklahoma wanted for the matter to be reconsidered and Joanna to be put on probation.

But that's another story.

•

Some of our congregational strife has been personal, not political. Joanna's predecessor, for example, became a target of grumbling. Some faulted the quality of her leadership and her sermon content and delivery. In fact, I'd initially voted against her hiring, because after hearing her deliver a sermon, I figured her writing wouldn't, in the long run, please our picky congregation. But after three years, the point at which she received a poor performance evaluation, I'd warmed up to her as a person.

Prior to an ill-spirited congregational meeting, I didn't know the discontent ran so deep in some. I'd heard snippets but I didn't know that a group of about 10 congregants had convinced themselves that firing her without a probationary period was the right next step.

At a long, painful meeting, I asked about Biblical precedents for hitting somebody in the head with a two-by-four, then setting the body on the curb. (To be honest, I didn't ask for scriptural citations, but I do remember the part about putting the body on the curb.) If you whack somebody in an evaluation, I argued, shouldn't you at least give her a chance to improve?

"By the way," I added, in nasty conclusion, "everything that's said here is on the record, as far as I'm concerned. If you're willing to say something aloud in this room, you should be willing to stand by it publicly."

Ultimately, the pastor got a probationary period of nine months, and her position was cut to three-quarters time. I tried to coach her in sermon-writing but eventually she quit, and we began to search for a half-time replacement. Our squabbles and subsequent loss of members had drawn down our bank account.

•

One Sunday, a youthful congregant, who with his family had dropped out of church for a time, sermonized about the wandering of the Israelites after their escape from Egypt. They received help from God, in the form of manna. There have been spells when I have wished for a downpour of manna to nourish our congregational spirit. I've watched us put on the armor of high principle and run at each other at top speed. (I include myself here.) I can find dynamics like that in a stadium or arena, or at a political gathering, but I don't go to church for sport. In fact, it's heartbreaking.

As I've already said, the beauty and difficulty of Mennonite decision-making is that ideally, it requires consensus. Article 16 of the *Mennonite Confession of Faith* declares, in a footnote: "Decision making by consensus is a way of coming to unity in the church (see Acts 15:22) . . . . The church listens carefully to all voices, majority and minority. Consensus is reached when the church has come to one mind on the matter, or when those who dissent have indicated that they do not wish to stand in the way of a group decision."

Under this system, as I've said before, one person can "block" the will of 40. Alternatively, one or two or five who oppose an action can "stand aside" during a vote, in effect abstaining so that the tribe can move on. The upside is that this model of decision-making gets around the inherent violence a majority can wreak on a minority in a democratic system; the downside is, as I mentioned earlier, that one bonkers person can theoretically hold a group hostage. The profundity of some contemporary rifts makes this possibility especially threatening. The heat of the moment warps the words that issue from our lips and distorts what we hear.

Why does this sort of thing happen in churches, of all places? Carl Dudley, director of the Hartford Institute for Religion Research, has said that "conflict is a synonym for congregation" in the United States. Almost one in four pastors is fired or forced to resign. "The most common reason Protestant pastors leave parish ministry is an experience of stressful conflict," wrote John Dart in *Christian Century* magazine, summarizing a 2002 survey of 963 ex-pastors from several denominations.

The inability of congregants to talk kindly, or at all, to each other about contemporary issues – to find a way to live with or mitigate their differences – is likely one of the reasons for a statistic released in July 2004 by the National Opinion Research Center at the University of Chicago. Between 1993 and 2002, the share of Americans calling themselves Protestant dropped from 63 to 52 percent – after years of remaining stable. In another survey, conducted by Trinity College in Hartford, Connecticut, between 1990 and 2008, the number of people labeling themselves "mainline Protestants" dropped from 19 percent to 13 percent.

•

Conflict is only one issue that makes church difficult. A question also arises about how to translate religious ideas and ideals into action. In a small church, it's hard to dodge responsibility, if only because when you don't help carry the load, it's more noticeable than in a large church. When hands are few, more is required of each. I itch for our church to render more service to the community. As it is, once a month, we prepare and serve casseroles and wash dishes at a kitchen for the homeless and impoverished. That's the one service we have consistently provided to the larger community since I've been going to Peace. Recently, whining to another person in the church about how little we do, she got defensive, reminding me that we sell Guatemalan-crafted goods during sidewalk sales and send the profits back to their makers. But there's plenty more to do, we agreed. I didn't admit that despite my retirement I haven't upped the ante of my contributions to organizations asking for volunteers.

With so little conventional service, in the churchy sense, on my resume, I have to reach to find much to boast about. As the presidential election of 2004 approached, for example, a spasm of civic guilt led me across the state line to Missouri on Saturdays to register African-American voters. The voting booth is one of the few places where rich and poor count equally. As I think about it, it seems like a Mennonite sort of thing to do, given the church's emphasis on social justice, though at the time it seemed a civic, not a sacred, duty.

One of the most interesting conversations I had was with an African-American Jehovah's Witness named Jerry Lindsay. He was impeccably dressed as he approached me standing outside a neighborhood grocery and seemed stunningly out of place in the poor neighborhood to which I'd been assigned that day. When asked, he said that Franklin D. Roosevelt was the greatest president of the 20th century. He had also liked George McGovern very well.

"Are you registered to vote?" I asked.

"No, I've never voted."

"Why not?"

"Because nothing will change human beings short of Christ's return to Earth."

It struck me as sad that an obviously thoughtful man, a college graduate with a sense of history, would absent himself from the voting booth – especially given the many churchgoers who are fervent about politics and who brandish opinions like terrible swift swords.

If Jesus were among us, would he register African Americans to vote? I don't know. If Jerry Lindsay is right, he wouldn't have to. His reappearance might be so transformative that political tribes would disappear and voting become moot.

•

Another form of spiritual action – one directed at changing myself – has been writing. At its worst, writing has sometimes been an act of self-justification, a way of setting history straight (that is, as *I* want it to be understood). At its best, though, it is an act of self-clarification; it both drives me deeper into myself and forces me to distance from myself, to be an honest-as-I-can-be presenter of myself as subject and object at the same time. Writing this book has helped me understand that forgiving others and viewing my own failings with compassion are work I need to do.

When Christ forgave at Golgotha despite the nails, the spear in the side, the vinegar-laden sop, the taunts, he was doing what comes unnaturally to mortals. It is ours to copy that example in the less dramatic moments of our small lives. What can be more important than to learn to lower our temperature when we feel ourselves approaching the boiling point? My first step back toward a Christian life, in the late 1980s, involved acknowledging my rage and owning up to the fact that my intensity, charming as it seemed (at times) to me, could suck all the air out of a room. Knowing ourselves – and especially our shadow selves – is a life's work. There are far more of us little devils than there are big ones – the Pol Pots and Moammar Gadhafis – and our hard words and misdeeds, small as they are, cumulatively account for much human suffering.

You can grasp your part in this by meditating, confiding in friends or, as I said before, writing.

•

The world is full of people who have a religious urge but can't seem to find a congenial vessel for it. They can't seem to find an –ism or an –ology that works. Some stop trying. Some become serial believers, skipping from sanctuary to sangha, from this practice to that. Maybe they throw together a spiritual casserole. Are you someone who has thrown a wistful glance from time to time in the direction of this or that spiritual practice . . . who has tried this or that church . . . this or that New Age practice . . . but then balked, embarrassed at what your friends might think if they found out? Did you throw away the familiar religious blueprints, as I did, long ago – but then find some circumstance nagging you to take a fresh look at the old verities? If so, I invite you to join me at a party (though I wasn't asked to host it) of those too stubborn to quit seeking and too hard-headed to be satisfied with either the big-guy-in-the-sky view of the religious or the cogs-and-gears view of the mechanist.

I invite you to sit Zen, praise Allah, study Torah. Will it be a pew or prayer rug? Incense, chants – or something simpler? You choose.

I chose, when I took up the business, to try Christianity again. It was my mother's religion, and I admired her: She lived it with quiet dignity. Its terms were familiar. Just so, I advise you take up a practice and follow a path that feels right to you or, perhaps, just bearable. If, as you sample, you sense that you're compromising your intellect or risking your integrity . . . or if you get attacks of vertigo . . . or find your new companions strange . . . or just feel creeped out, then pull back. Mumbling a prayer of thanks or petition now and again may be enough religion for you. Or strolling through a stand of giant sequoias.

That is, take what you want and leave the rest.

Perhaps God, metaphorically, is the sun and some of us are plants with a tropism for God, destined to turn only slowly, in the course of that long day called a lifetime, toward the sun. Proceed at your own chosen speed. There's just one rule I'd suggest, the meta-rule enunciated by Christ and repeated in Leviticus, Matthew, Mark, Luke, Roman, Galatians, James: Love your neighbor as yourself. That means forgiving the frailty of both.

Some will say you *must* believe in the atonement of Jesus Christ or the virgin birth . . . in the literal truth of the Bible . . . or the satanic nature of Howard Stern. A very few will strap on bombs to detonate themselves and other people or kill doctors who perform abortions. These few seem sure that Satan is as real as God, and working among us, so that they MUST act, with swift, harsh conviction, to check the demonic.

I don't share this certainty, but it is one face of religion today, and good people use it to attack religion. It gives doubters a rationale to stay away. The number of Americans reporting NO religious preference doubled, from 7 to 14 percent, in the 1990s, according to a study conducted by Michael Hout and Claude Fisher, of the University of California/Berkeley, and reported in *American Sociological Review*. The withdrawal of 5 to 7 percent from declaring a religious preference was a "political act," they wrote, "a dissent from the affinity that had emerged between conservative politics and organized religion."

I offer this thought: If the social agenda of the spiritual body you grew up in seems off-kilter, alternatives other than retreat do exist. For example, if you believe that loving yourself and your neighbor is the business at hand, and if you believe that some of those in your first religious group need a reminder of this, then go home and, in a loving way, share this belief. It's a life's work trying to figure out how, in fact, to do this. You may fail. We all may. But go ahead: Act **as if** God exists and then act **as if** you love yourself and others, demanding of yourself an integrity that is humble, a plainspokenness that isn't mean, a willingness to challenge your first thought.

It's not complicated. It's just hard to pull off.

One of the comforts I have taken in returning to church after 30 years away is that now I'm the old one. The body chemistry that drove my certainty has changed. Perhaps it's my turn to have a little influence. I figure with things going as badly as they are, I can risk saying this:

Take from sacred text, from church, from prayer, from fellow congregants, what you need, what nourishes. There are many churches, each with its own character. There is a church for those called to public service, a church for those with grief to dissolve, a church for those with war to protest, a church for those who would decode sacred text, a church for those who love the look of vestments or the smell of incense or the transport of song, a church for those who want a capsule of silence within which to ponder, a church for those who'd like to find a mate. Many needs arise within our lives, and religion exists to help us meet them, not to terrify or exclude, overwhelm or intimidate. The church also belongs to you – and you may bring something rare or missing, and altogether necessary, to it.

•

Finally, there's this from our amazing grace files.

One Sunday in July several years ago, a newcomer named George led the service. His partner, Mike, played our wretched piano.

In my time at Peace, we had never had, before that Sunday, a gay couple volunteer to lead a service.

My pal Jason, who was studying the philosopher Charles Sanders Peirce at the time and vexes my friend Steve with his want of belief in the atonement, was to have performed the prelude that morning. But then his wife, Rebecca, whose scholarly interest was Christian romance novels, gave birth to an 8 pound 12 ounce baby boy. So the prelude came not from Jason but a boom box sitting on top of the piano.

The sermon by George, who left a church in Texas after coming out, was about the Lord's Prayer. I mean the *real* Lord's prayer – which is to say the one I remember hearing as a boy, not the New Zealand version or a version drafted, say, by a cool blogger. As part of the service, the hymn version of the prayer was sung. A more beautiful soprano voice I'd never heard at Peace, its owner a friend of the two men, their gift, and hers, to us on this particular morning.

We sang the Doxology – "Praise God from whom all blessings flow" – another childhood standard. Mennonites are understandably proud of their gift for singing in four-part harmony. These outcroppings of the old-time religion had me reeling. *What are the Zennonites thinking about all this?* I wondered. At the end of the service, we prayed the Lord's Prayer aloud together. It was the first time in years I'd heard the old, familiar words. It took a gay man, someone not ordained (but who was just about to finish his master's in theology), to lead the most liturgically conventional service I'd ever experienced at Peace Mennonite.

Those fabled mysterious ways of God? Who knows.

I sat behind Steve, my fellow Sunday school teacher, and I saw him take off his glasses after the Lord's prayer. Steve, who had the courage to stay at the church even though he was outtalked, outnumbered and outvoted when it came to the welcoming statement, was teary.

The next day I saw Steve's wife, Eileen, in the driveway outside her house.

"Wasn't that service yesterday beautiful?" she said.

"I cried."

"Steve loved it." We both smiled.

The two men, by the way, left our congregation soon after. We weren't nearly conservative enough for them.

God is great.

ACKNOWLEDGEMENT

Phillip Lopate led a writer's workshop I attended in the early 2000s. One of my essays offended some of my classmates. So I asked how to make my shortcomings more palatable on the page.

Phillip said that a memoirist who wanted to reach an audience beyond his family and loved ones had to "shine a light into his own shadows. Help us see the monster in you more clearly. Think against yourself."

I thank him for that and other wisdom he shared.

Doug Koch

Roger Martin edited *Explore*, a University of Kansas research magazine that won 12 national awards in 14 years. In 1990 a panel of *Newsweek* jurors named it one of the nation's 10 best college/university magazines. In 1995 he began to write commentaries about KU research that were broadcast on Kansas Public Radio and published in several Kansas newspapers. In addition, Martin co-edited an oral history about hippy life in Lawrence, Kansas, *Cows Are Freaky When They Look at You: An Oral History of the Kaw Valley Hemp Pickers*, published by Watermark Press, Wichita, Kan., in 1991.

www.ingramcontent.com/pod-product-compliance
Lightning Source LLC
LaVergne TN
LVHW091040080826
845145LV00002B/571

9780990812838